Christmas Guitar Portraits

Duets for Two Acoustic Guitars

WILLIAM BAY MUSIC

Forward

The Christmas season has always been special to me. It is a season that has crystalized the hopes, aspirations and faith of millions of people through the centuries. The amount of music written for Christmas is monumental. This book contains 14 scores from my recording of the same title. I selected various genres dear to me. First, there are selections from the early American sacred song tradition. *The Babe of Bethlehem, Cherry Tree Carol, A Star in the East, The Shepherd's Star, A Virgin Unspotted* and *I Wonder As I Wander** all are from this rich heritage. I also picked a number of carols from the "Old English" genre. *Away In The Manger, Green Grow'th the Holly* and *What Child is This* are included. Then there are the Christmas favorites. *In the Bleak Mid-winter* and a medley of *Baloo, Lammy; The First Noel* and *Silent Night* make any Christmas complete. *Let All Mortal Flesh Keep Silence* is one of my favorite Advent hymns. *Gaudete, Christus est natus* is a rousing carol dating back many centuries. Finally, I included two originals. *Lullay, My Liking* is an ancient carol text. Many composers over the centuries have written melodies to these lyrics, most notably Gustav Holst. I could not resist the temptation so the melody here is original. Finally, *Christmas Prayer* is a new composition written for this recording.

I have always wanted to compose and arrange music designed to bring the plectrum or flatpick guitar to the concert stage. These arrangements were written with that in mind.

Some of the arrangements call for a low A or B note as played on a 7 string guitar. These can easily be replaced by a low A or B pedal note as found on a 6 string guitar.

I would also recommend my prior recording entitled **Acoustic Guitar Portraits**. The scores for that duo collection are also available. Finally, I have an extensive recording of concert solos for plectrum guitar called **Guitar Images**. The scores for each of those original solos are available in the **Guitar Images** book.

William Bay

Contents

Composition	Page Number

The Babe of Bethlehem

Early American Carol

William Bay

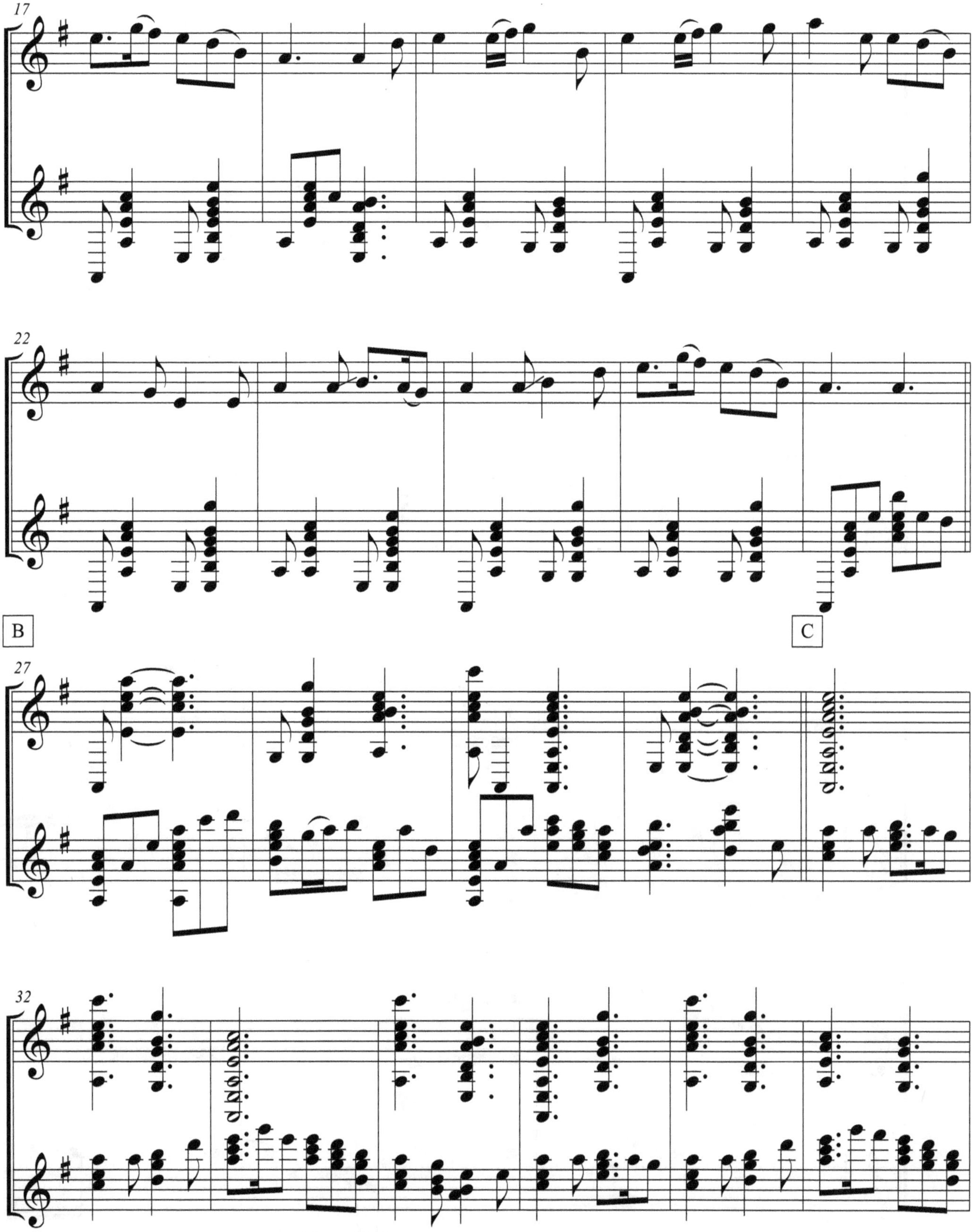
17
22
B
C
27
32

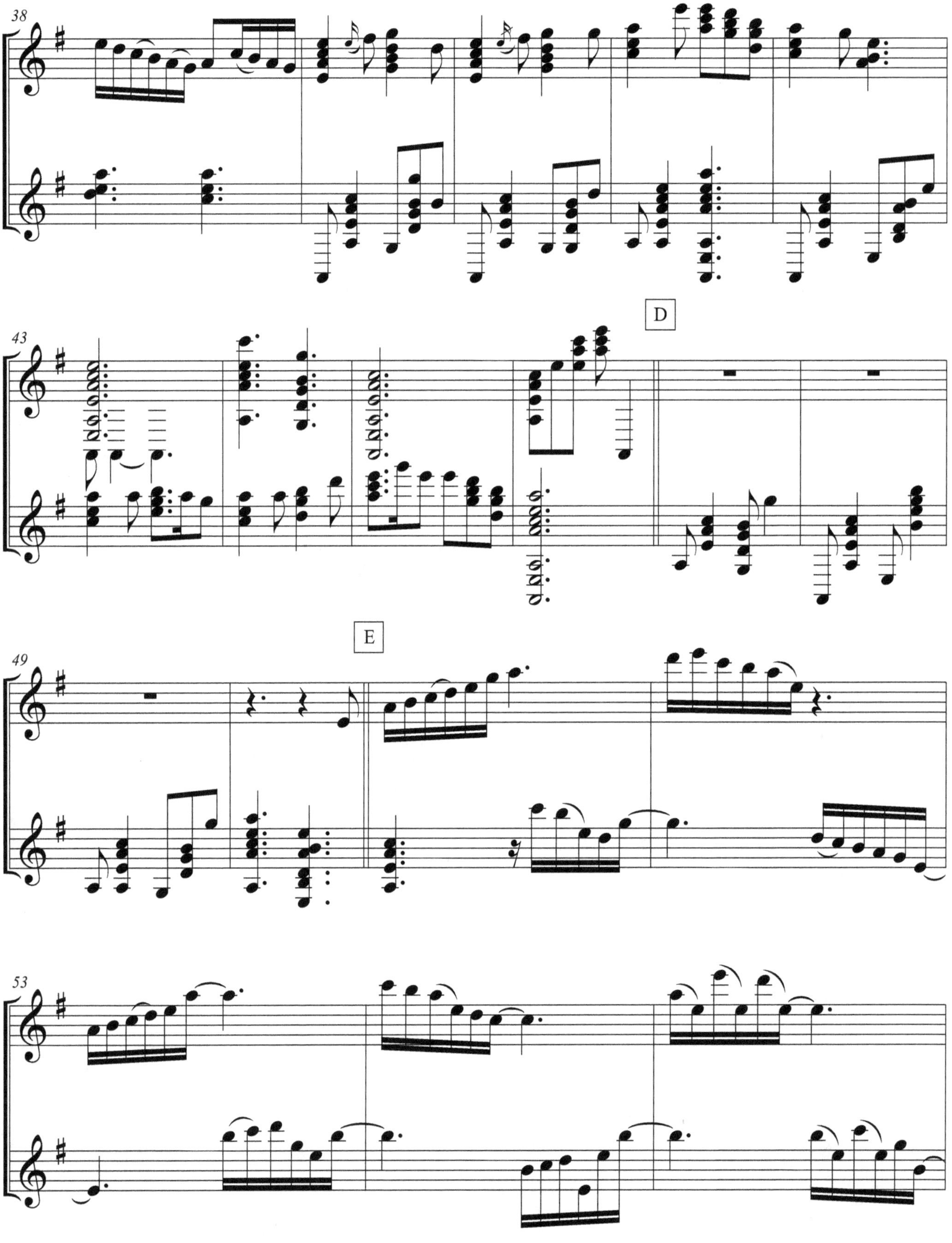
38
43
D
49
E
53

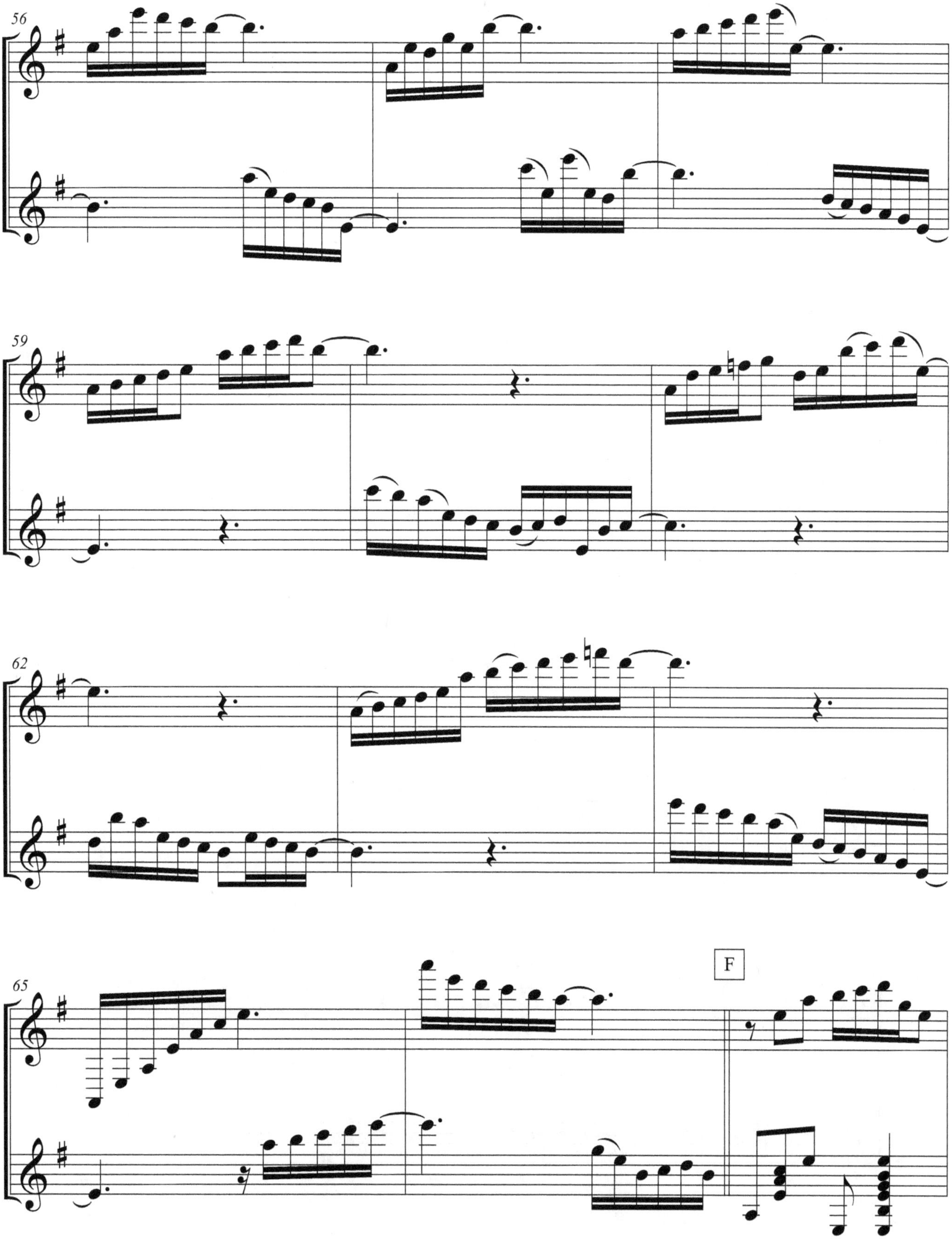
56
59
62
65
F

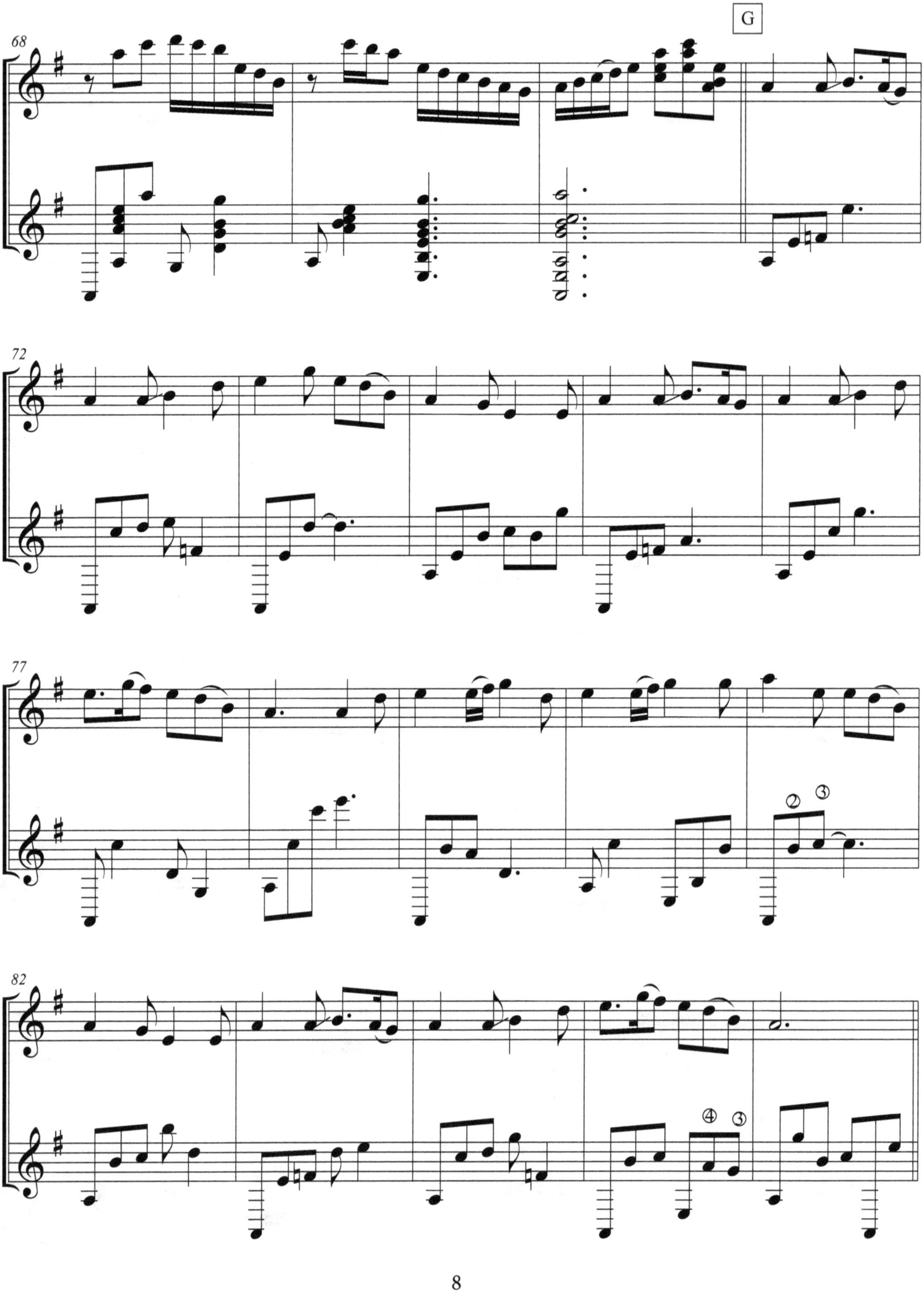
68
G
72
77
82

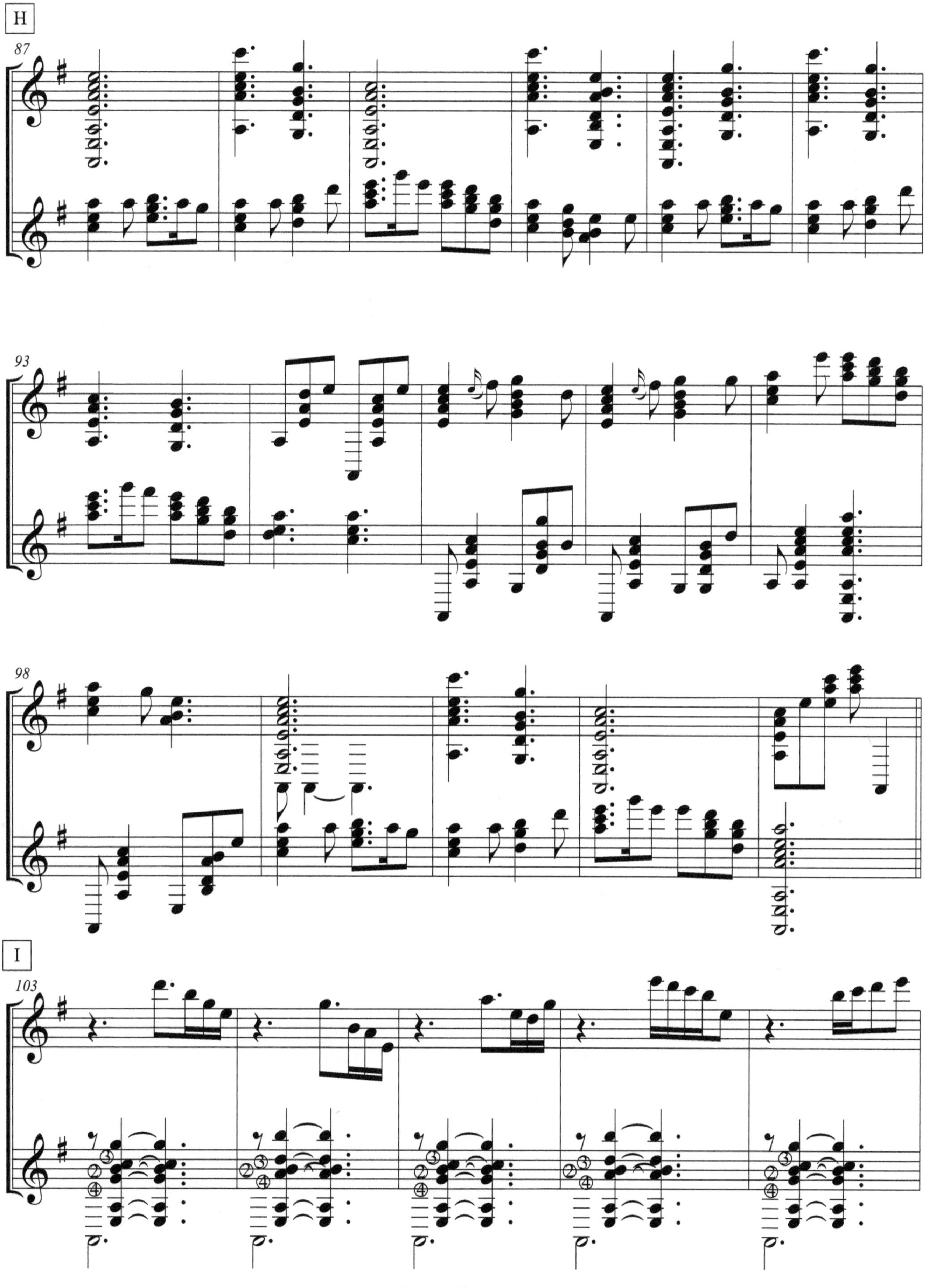
H
87
93
98
I
103

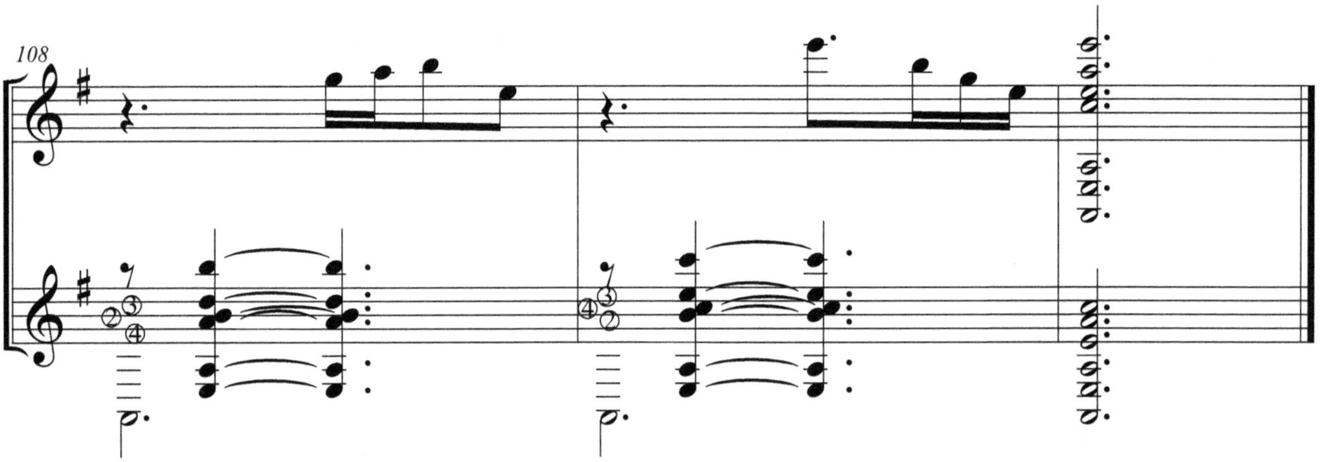
108

The Cherry Tree Carol

Dropped D Tuning

Early American Carol

William Bay

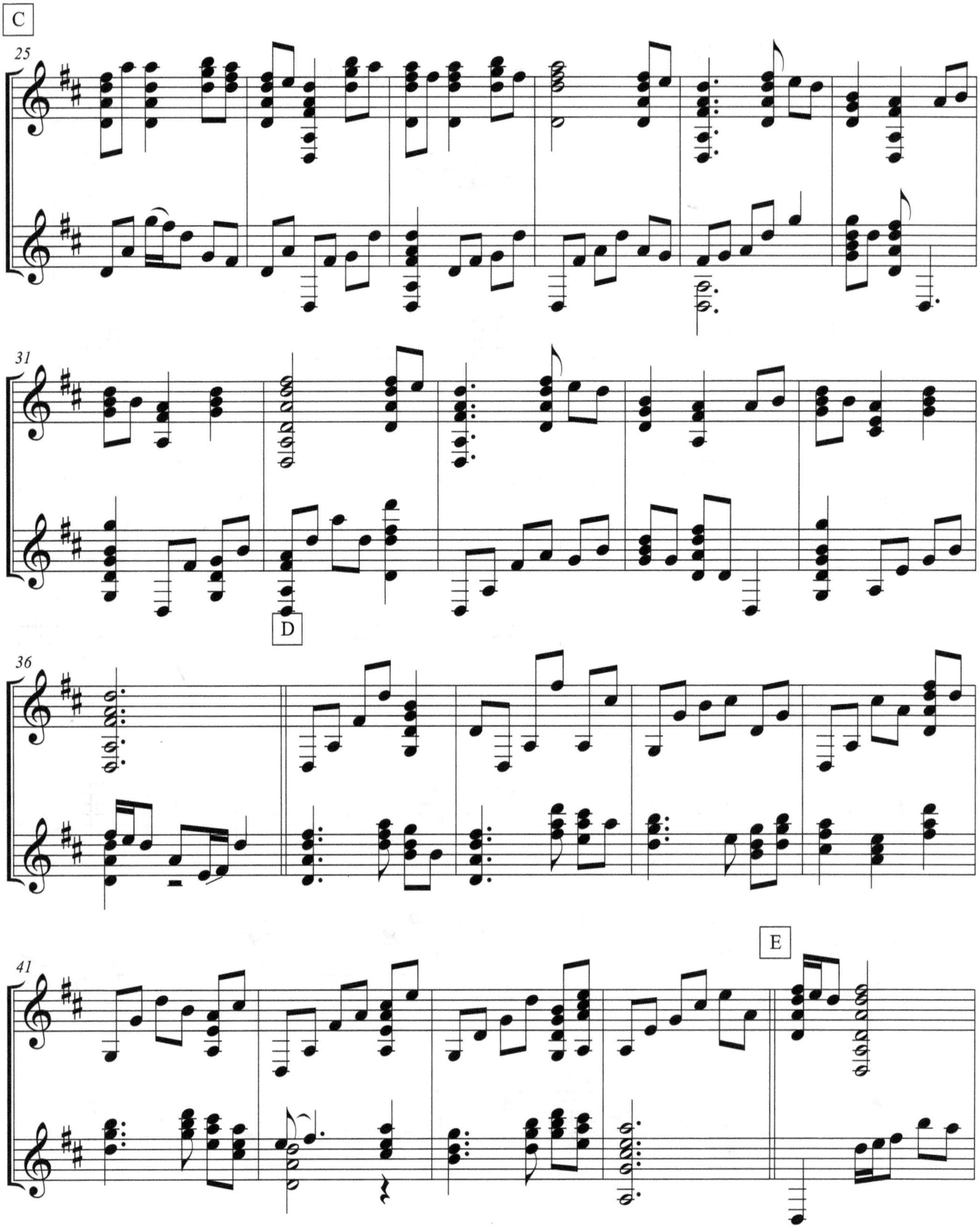
C
25
31
D
36
41
E

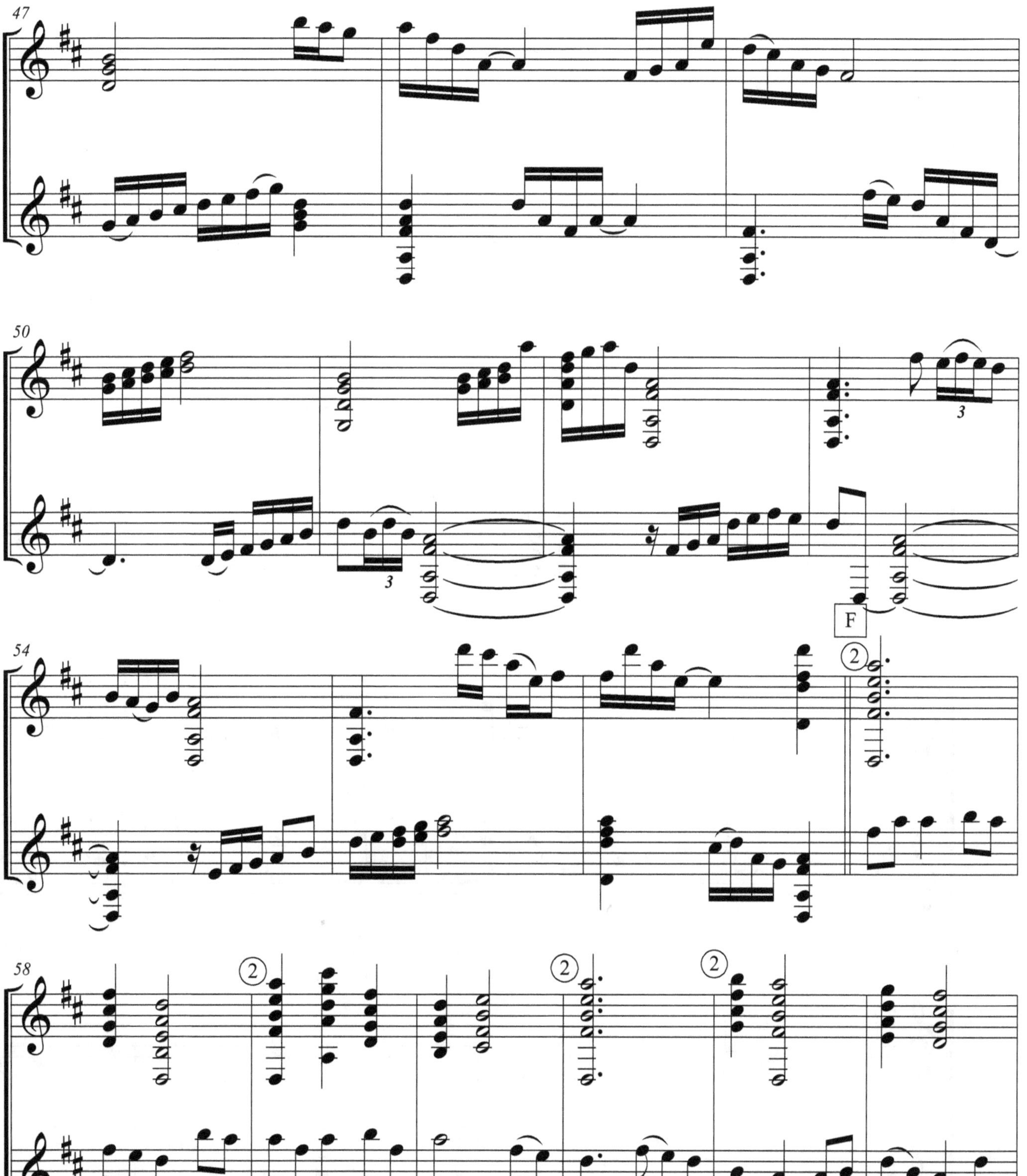
47
50
3
3
54
F
2
58
2
2
2

14

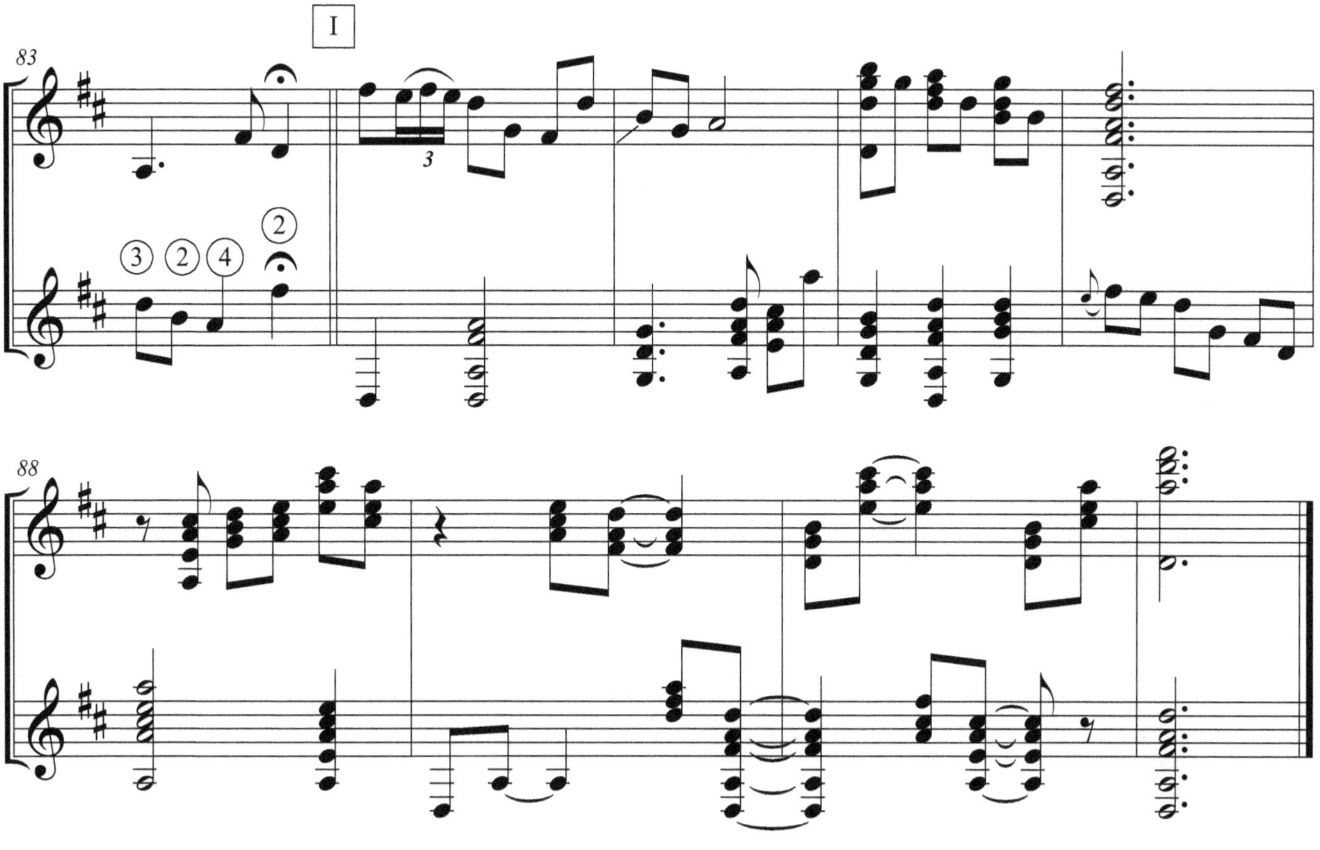
83
I
88

In The Bleak Mid-winter

Dropped D Tuning

Gustav Holst
arr. by William Bay

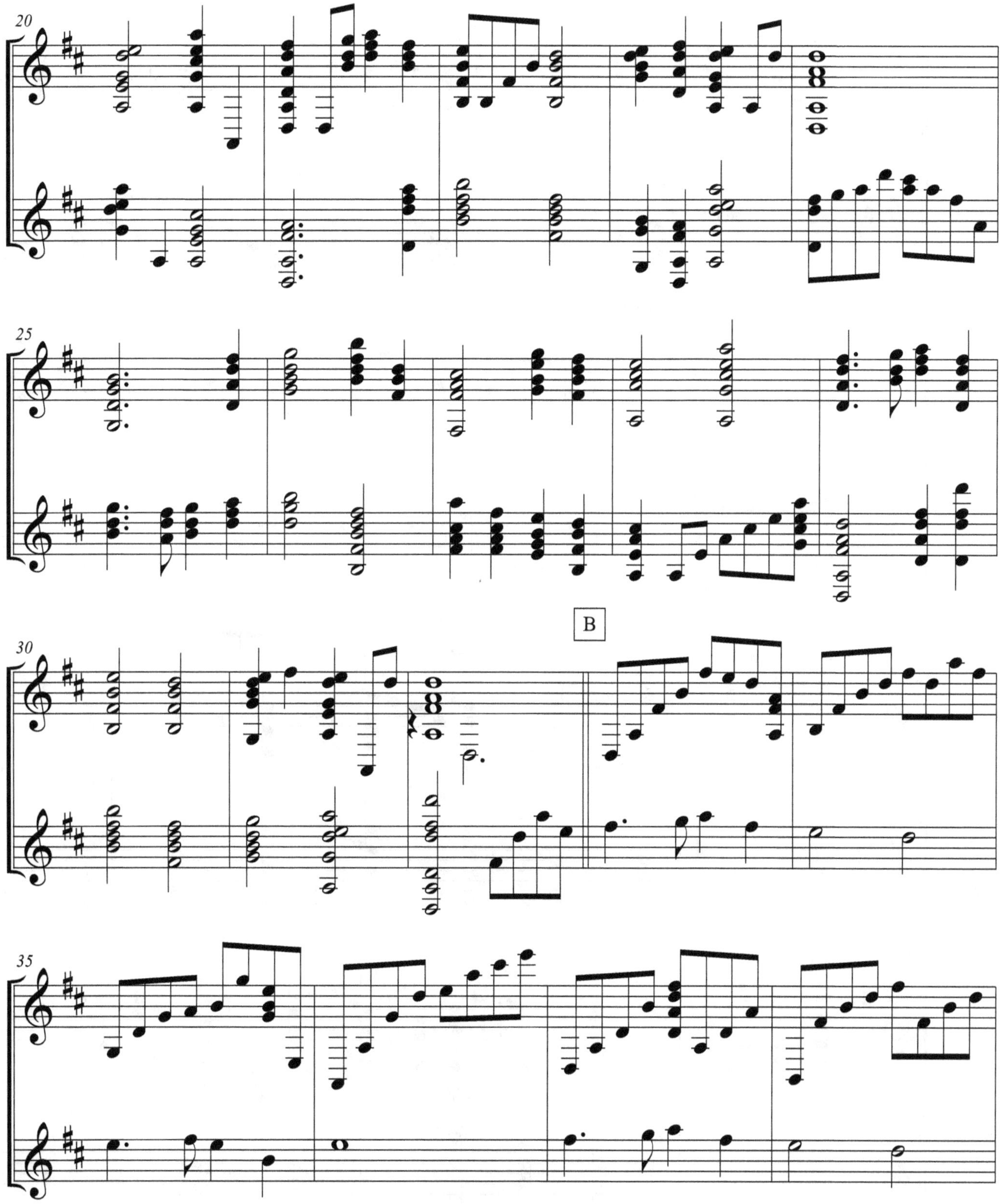
20
25
30
B
35

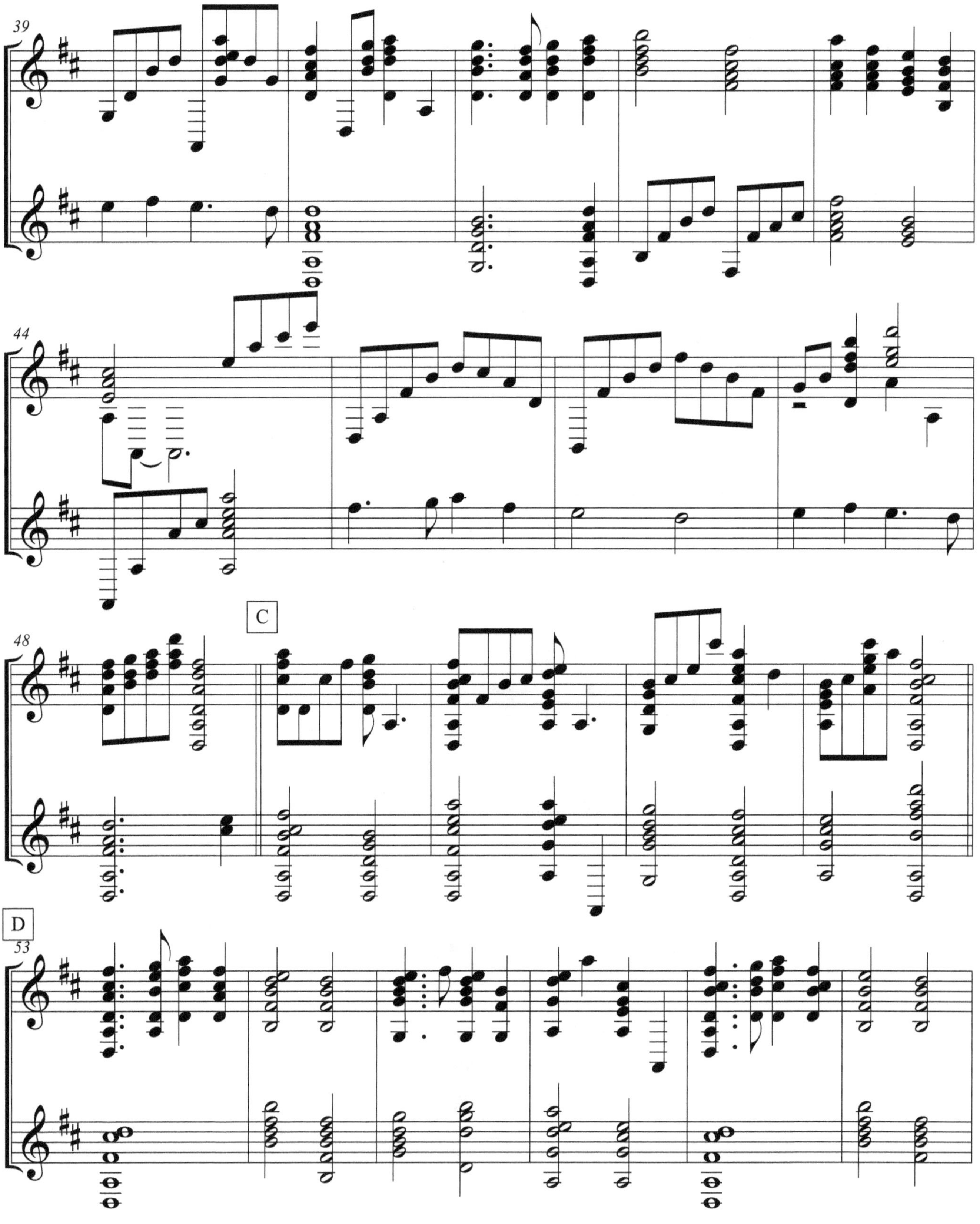
39
44
48
C
D
53

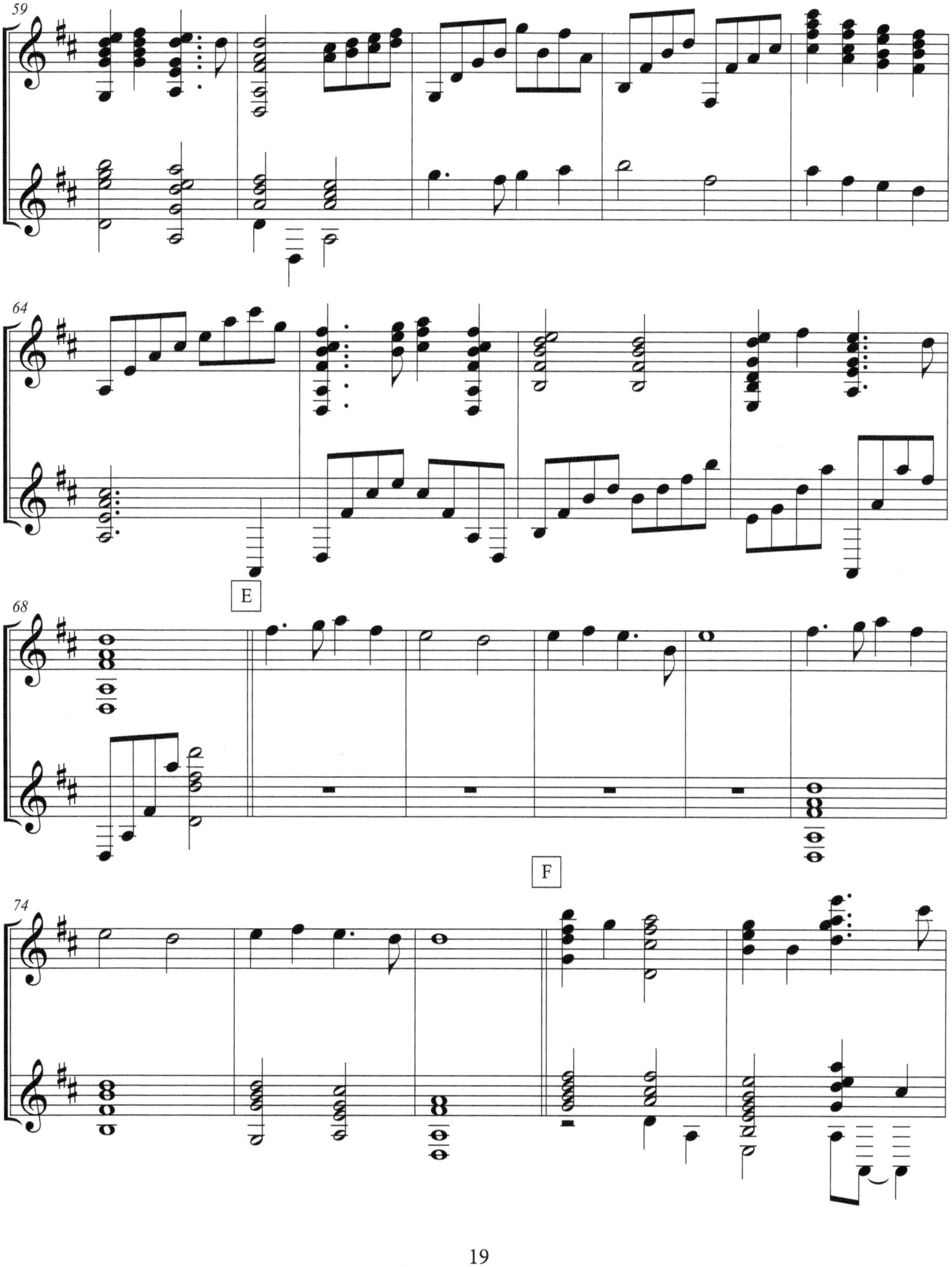
59
64
E
68
F
74

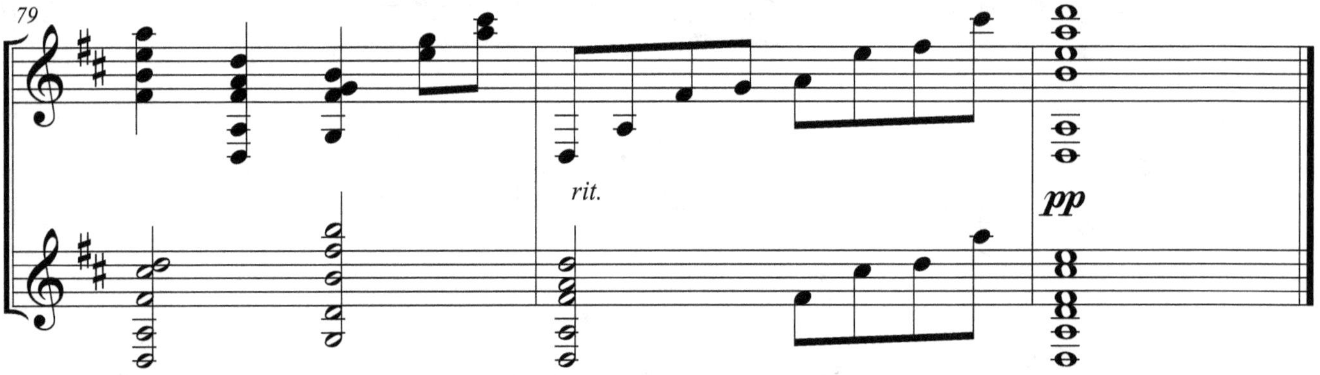
79
rit.
pp

A Star In The East

Early American Carol

William Bay

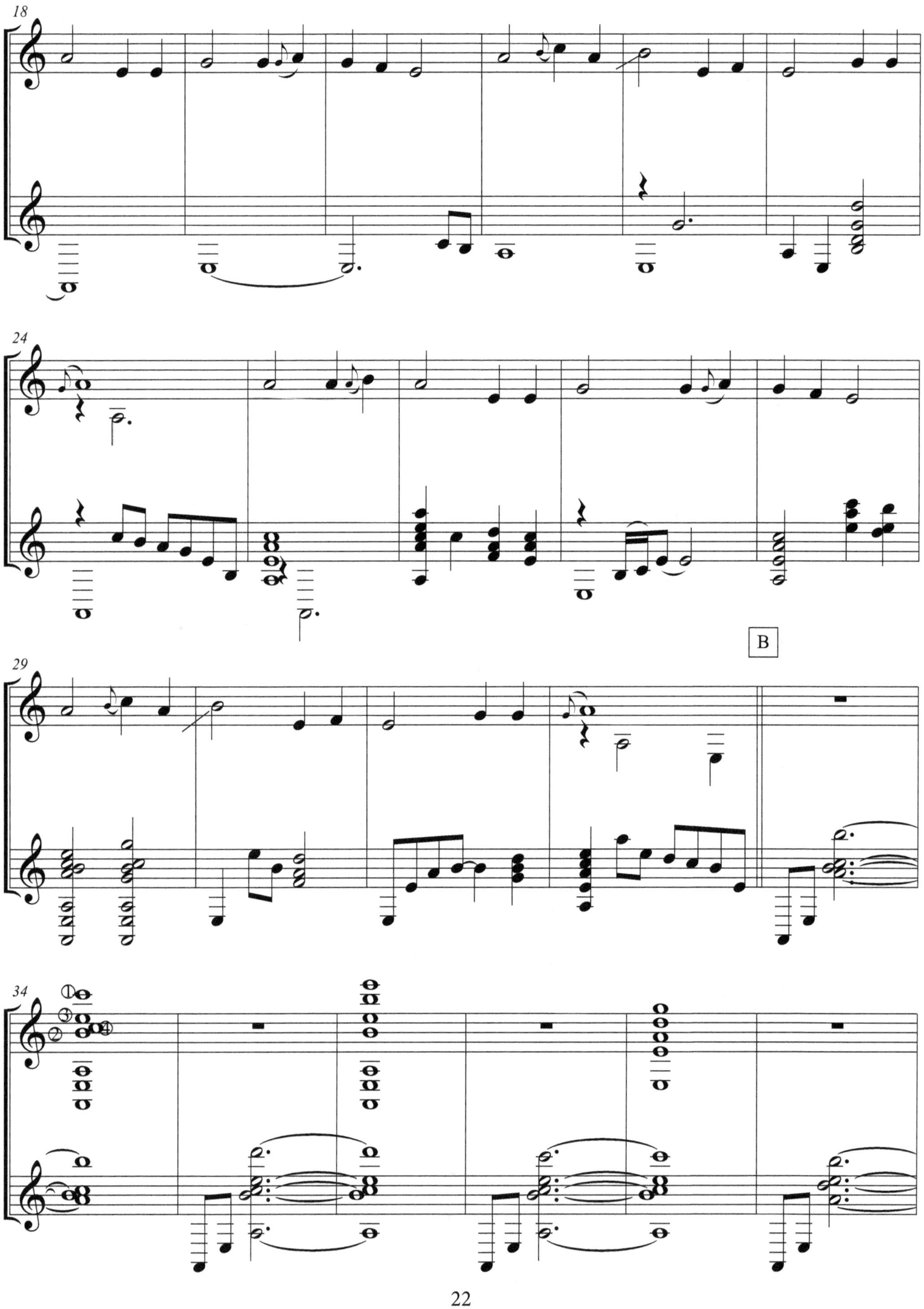
18
24
29
B
34
① ③ ② ④

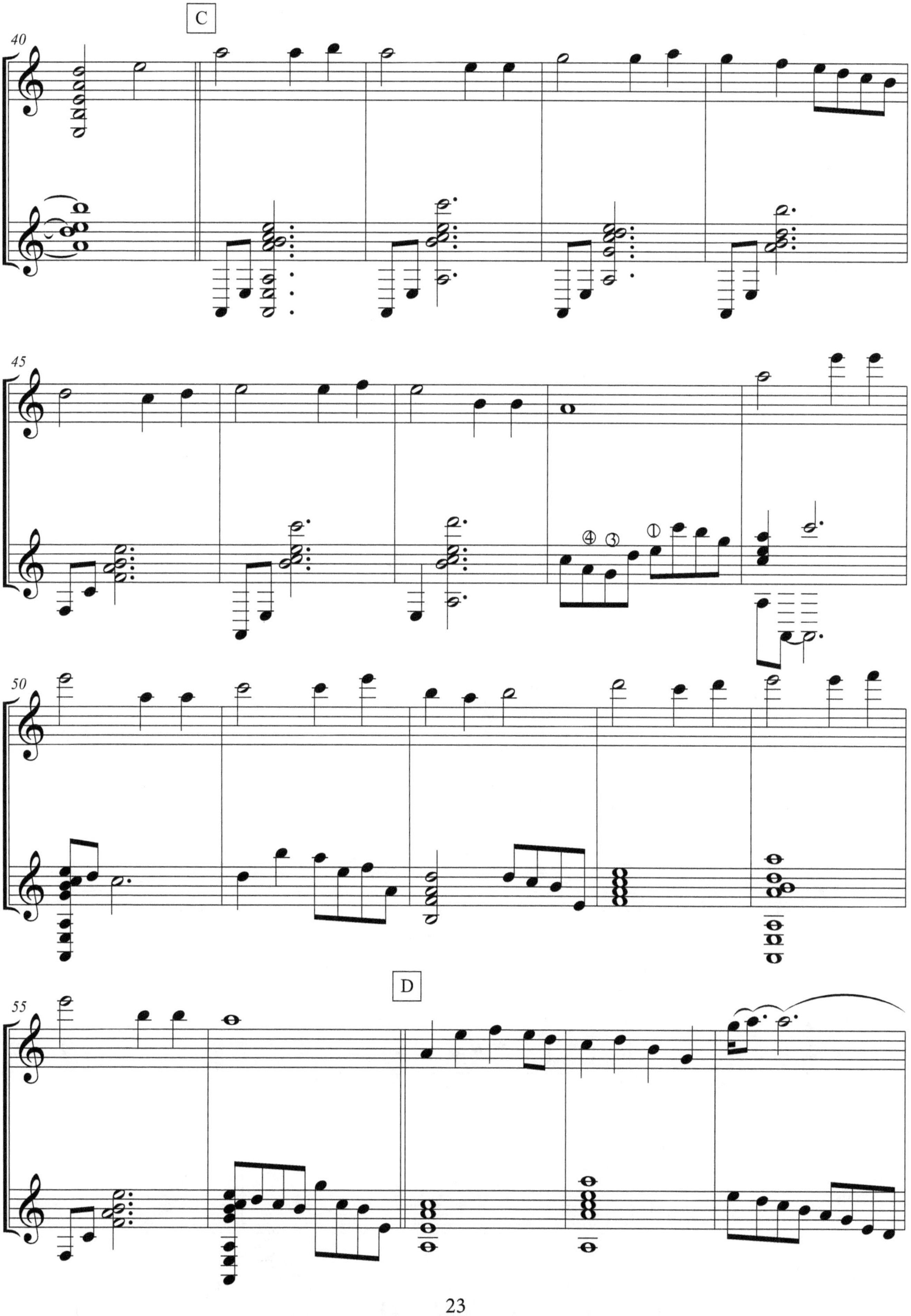
C
40
45
④ ③ ①
50
55
D

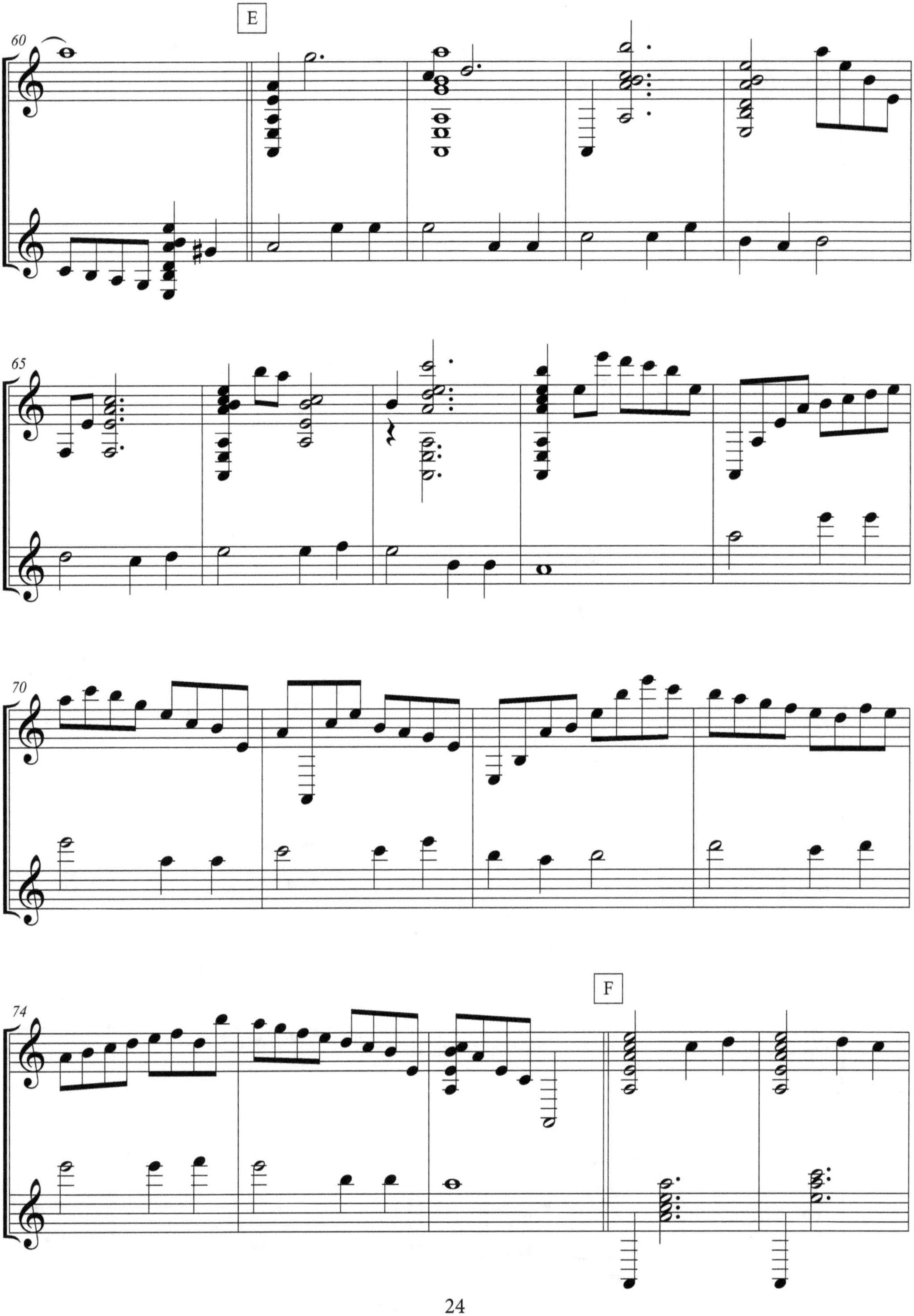
60
E
65
70
74
F

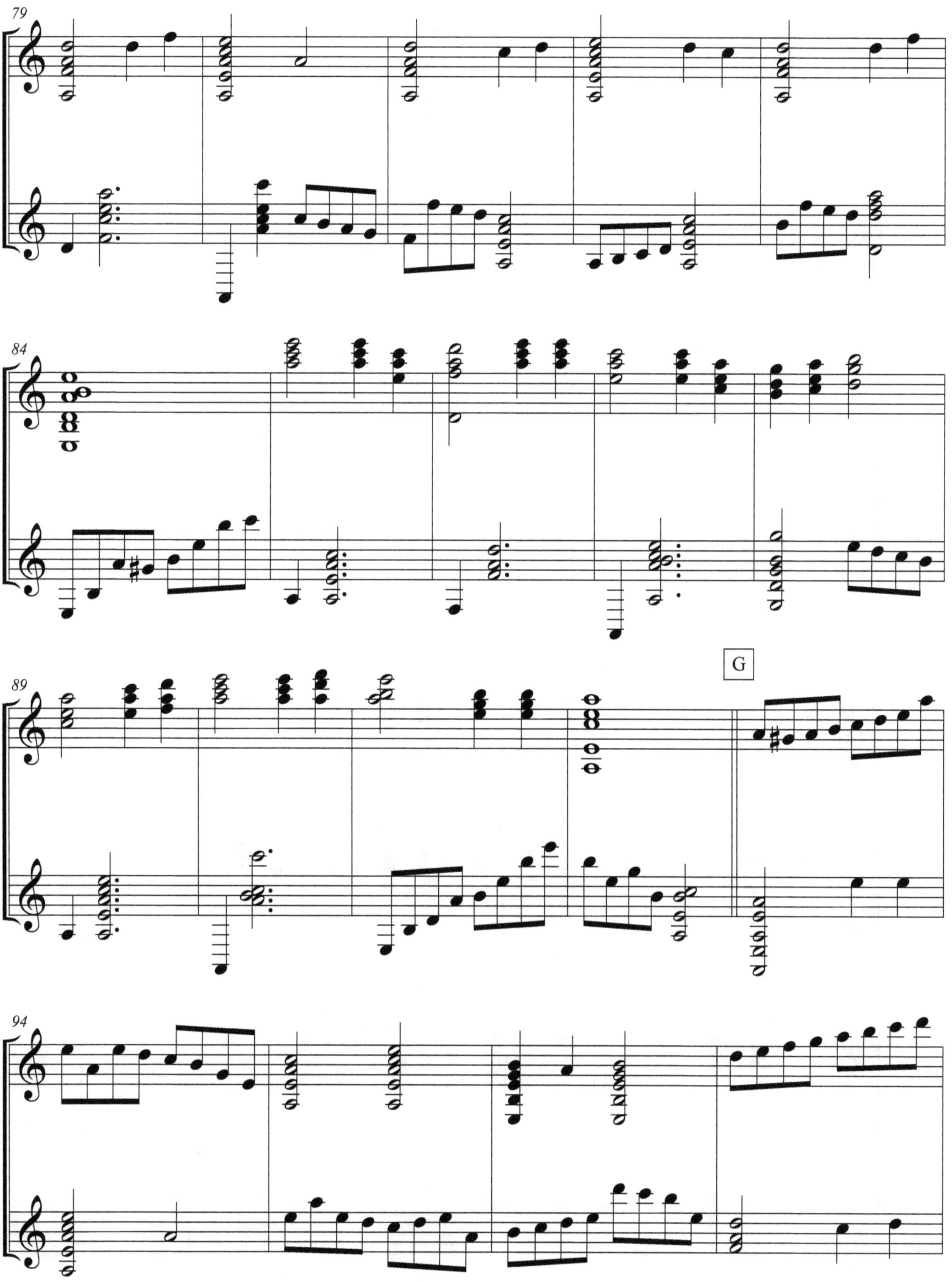
79
84
89
G
94

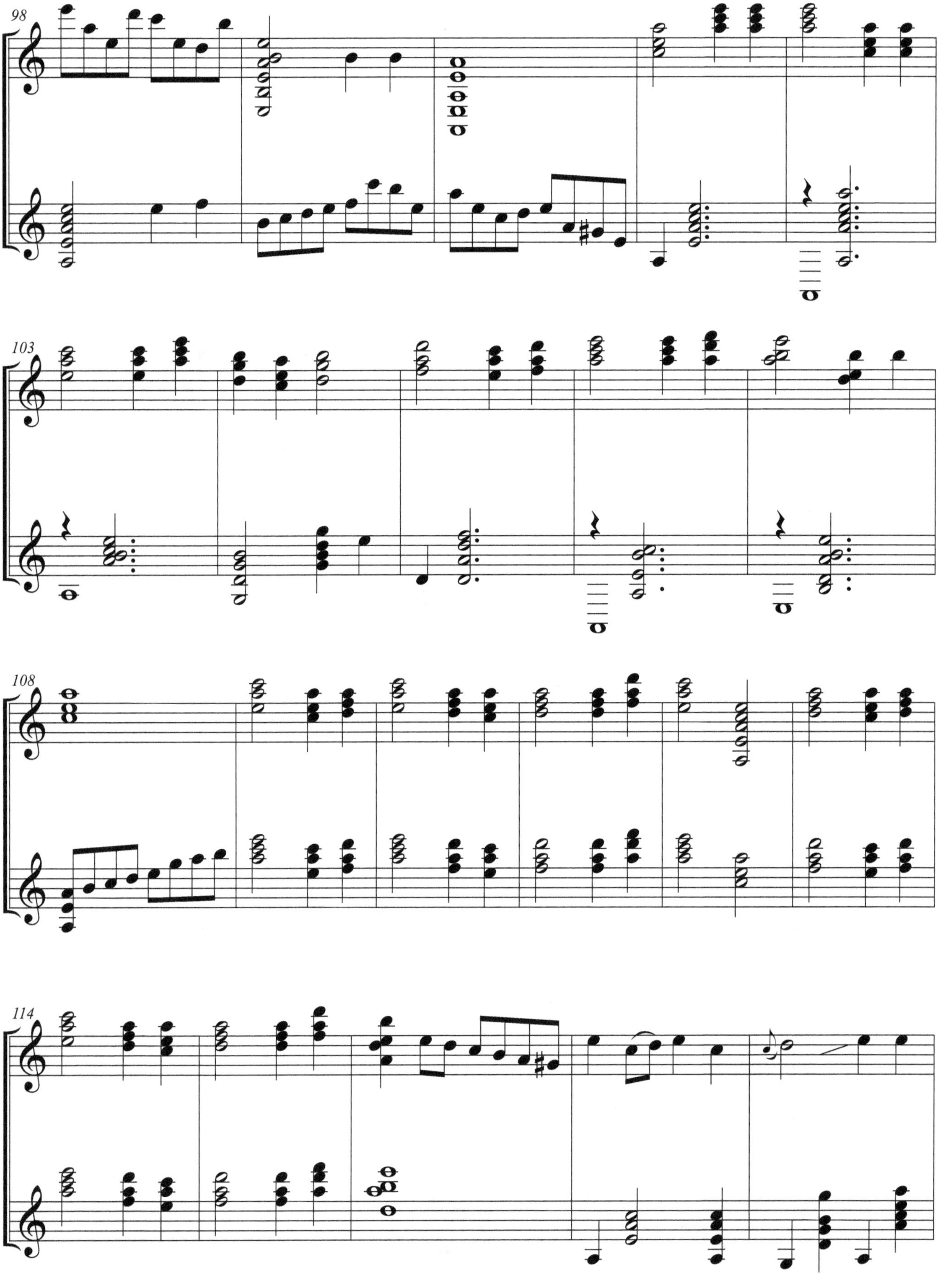
98
103
108
114

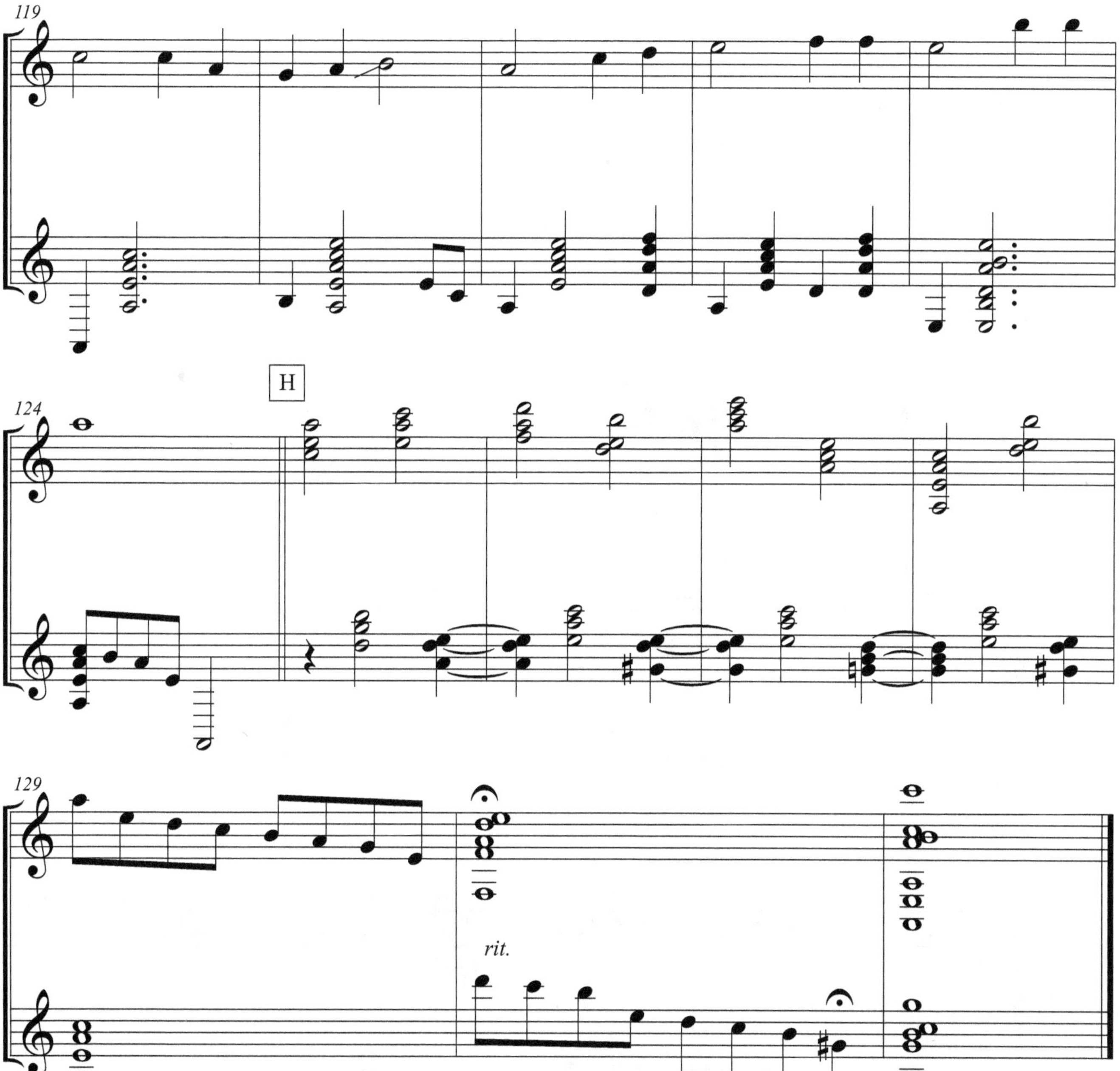
119
124
H
129
rit.

Let All Mortal Flesh Keep Silence

Dropped D Tuning

arr. by William Bay

♩ = 52

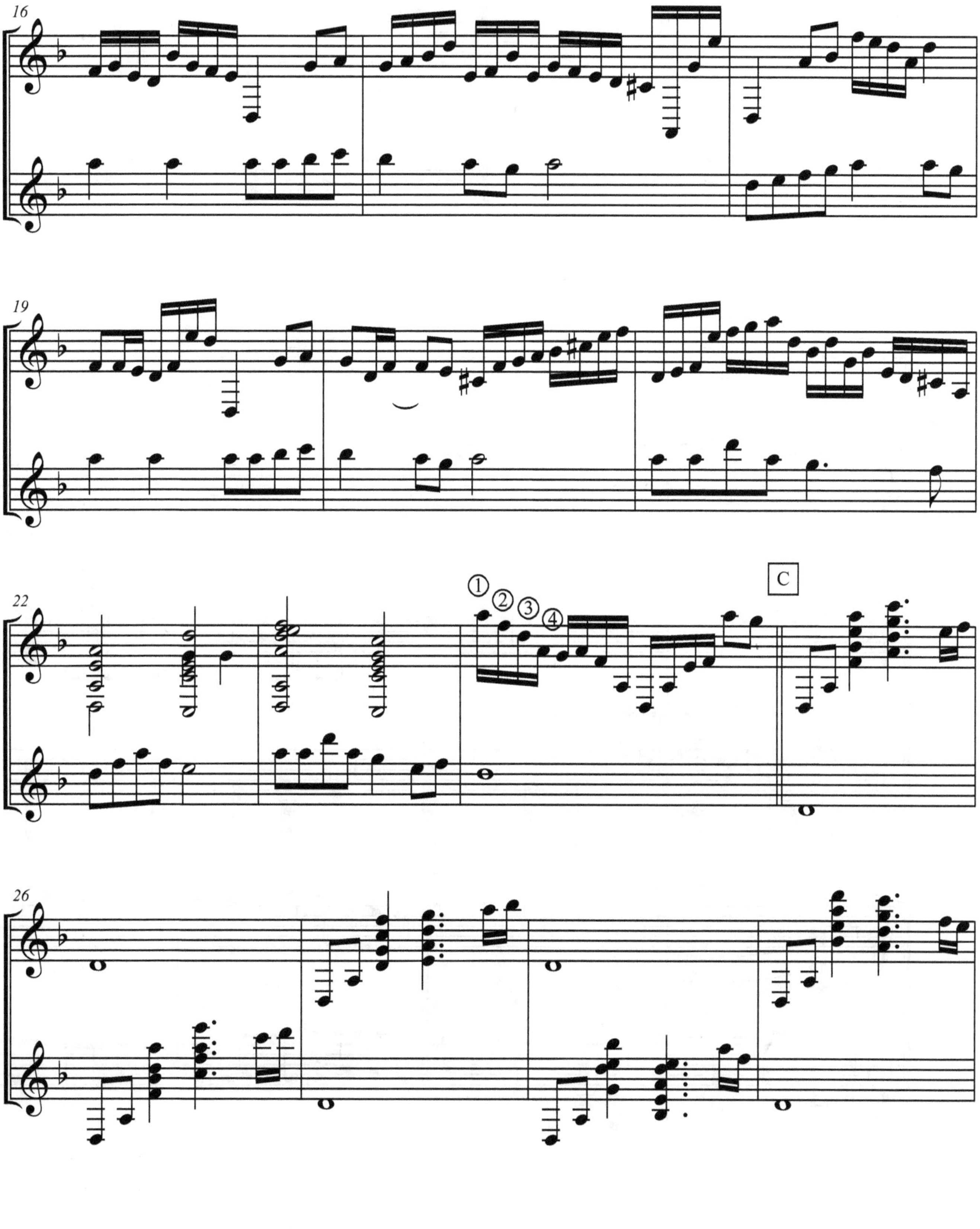
16
19
22
①
②
③
④
C
26

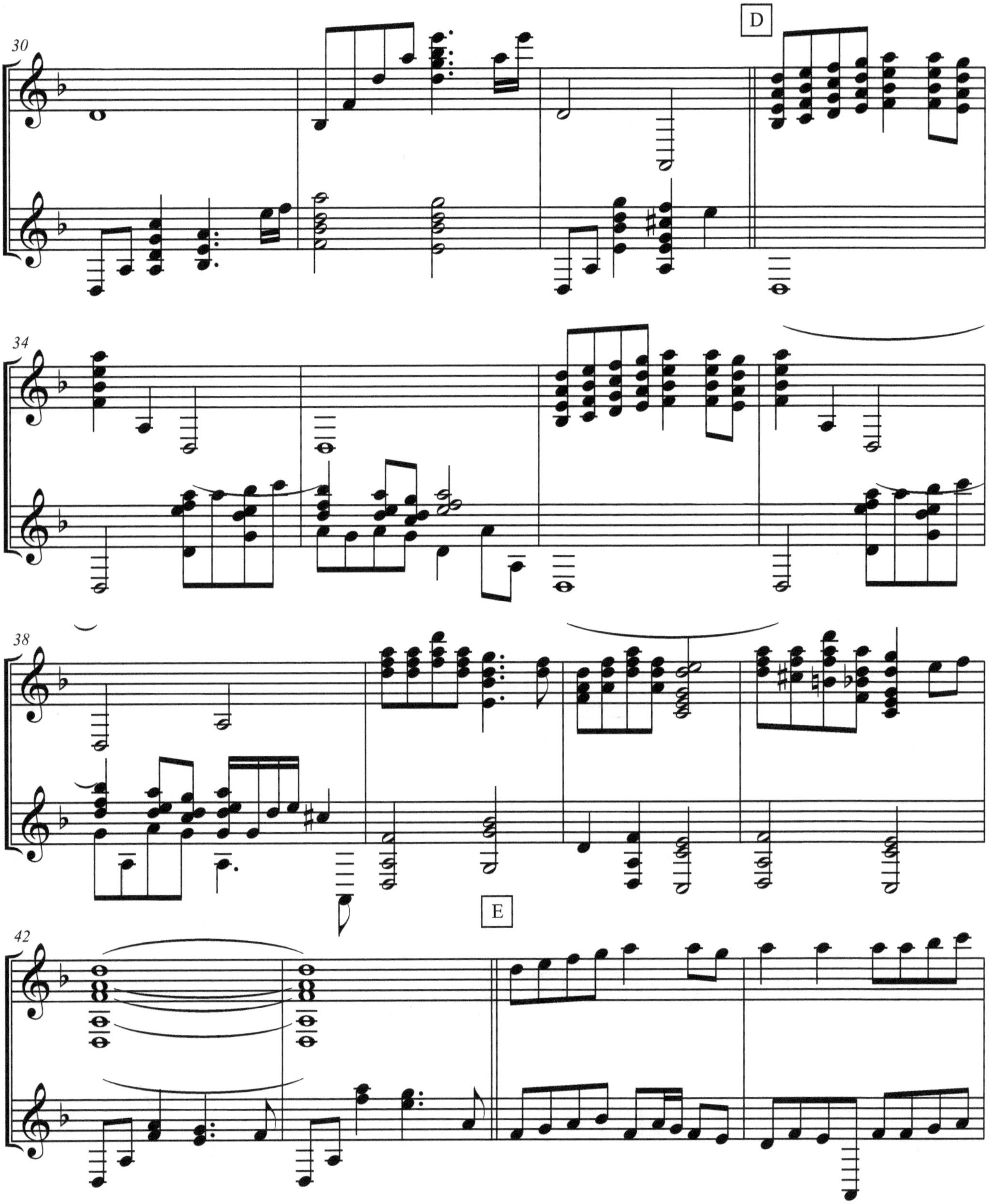
30
D
34
38
42
E

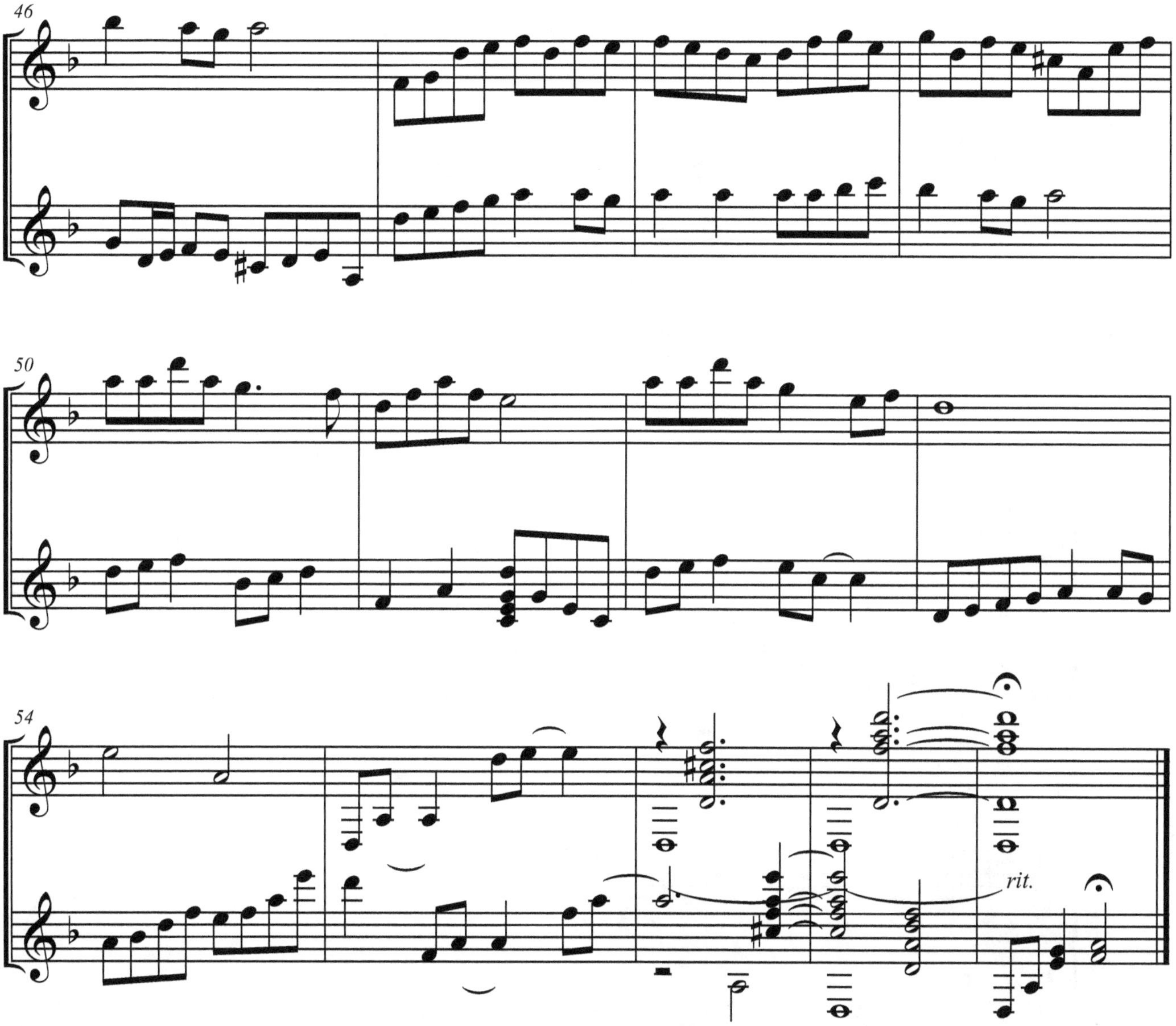
46
50
54
rit.

Away In The Manger

Dropped D Tuning

English Version

Arranged by William Bay

Slowly

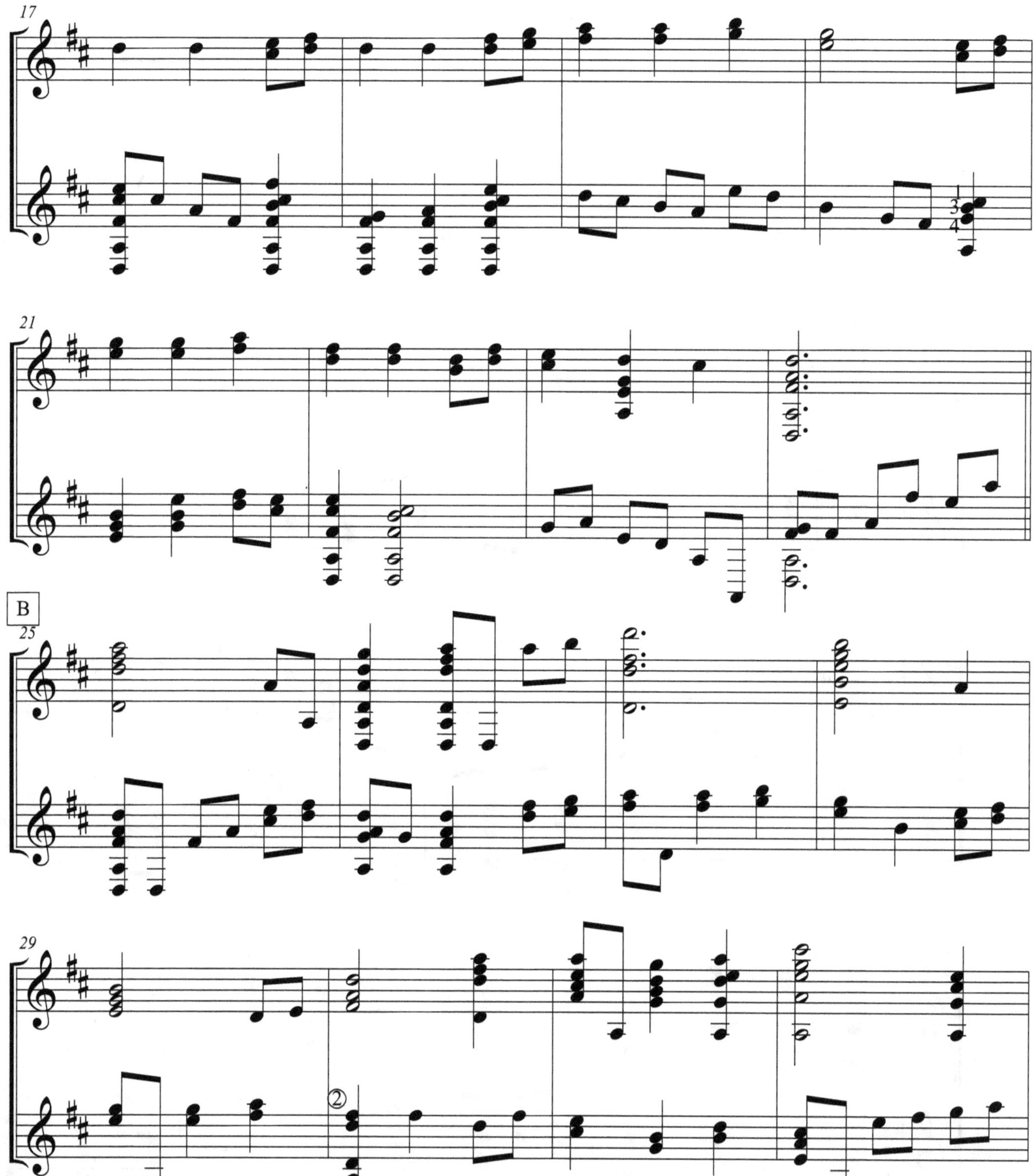
17
21
B
25
29

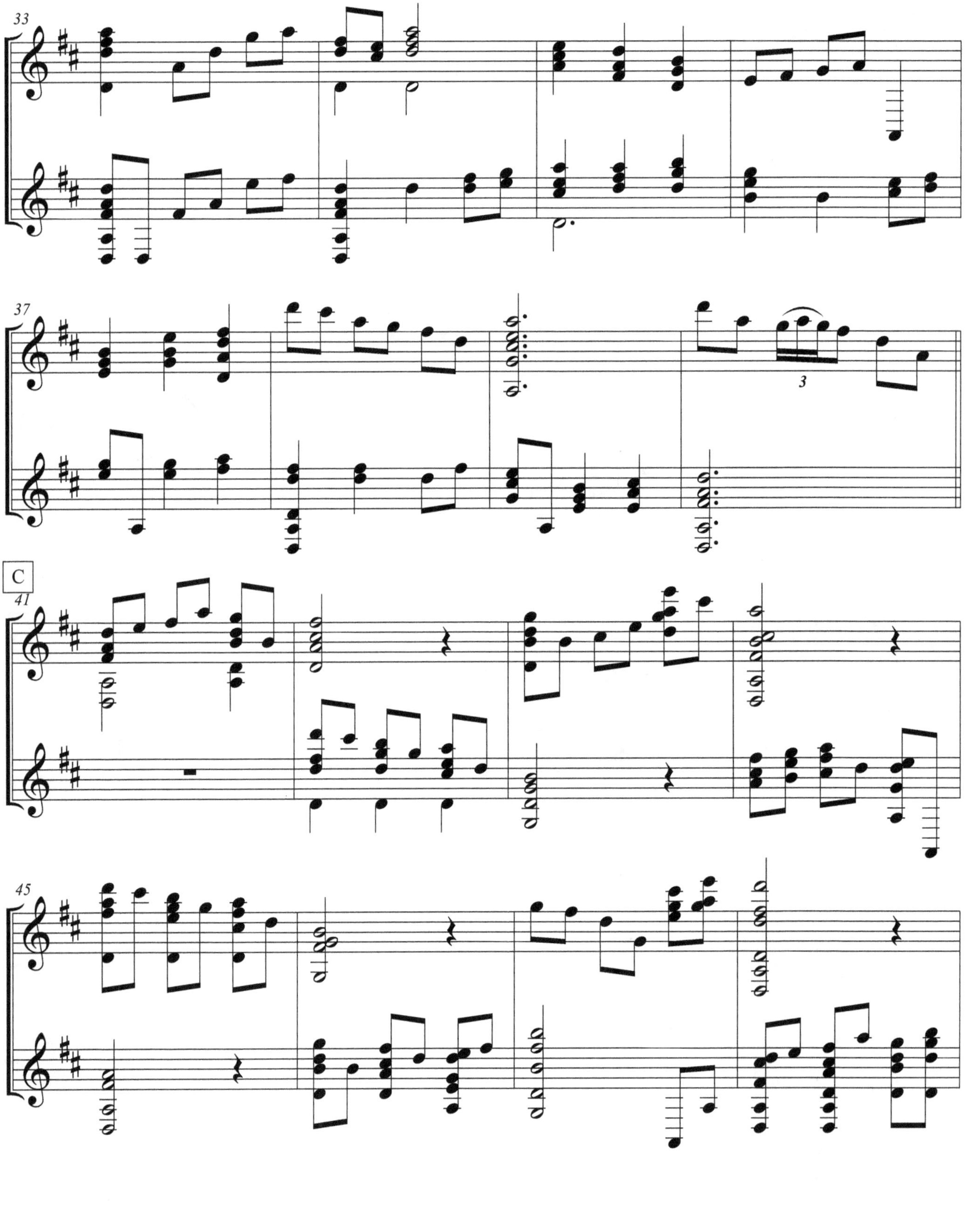
33
37
3
C
41
45

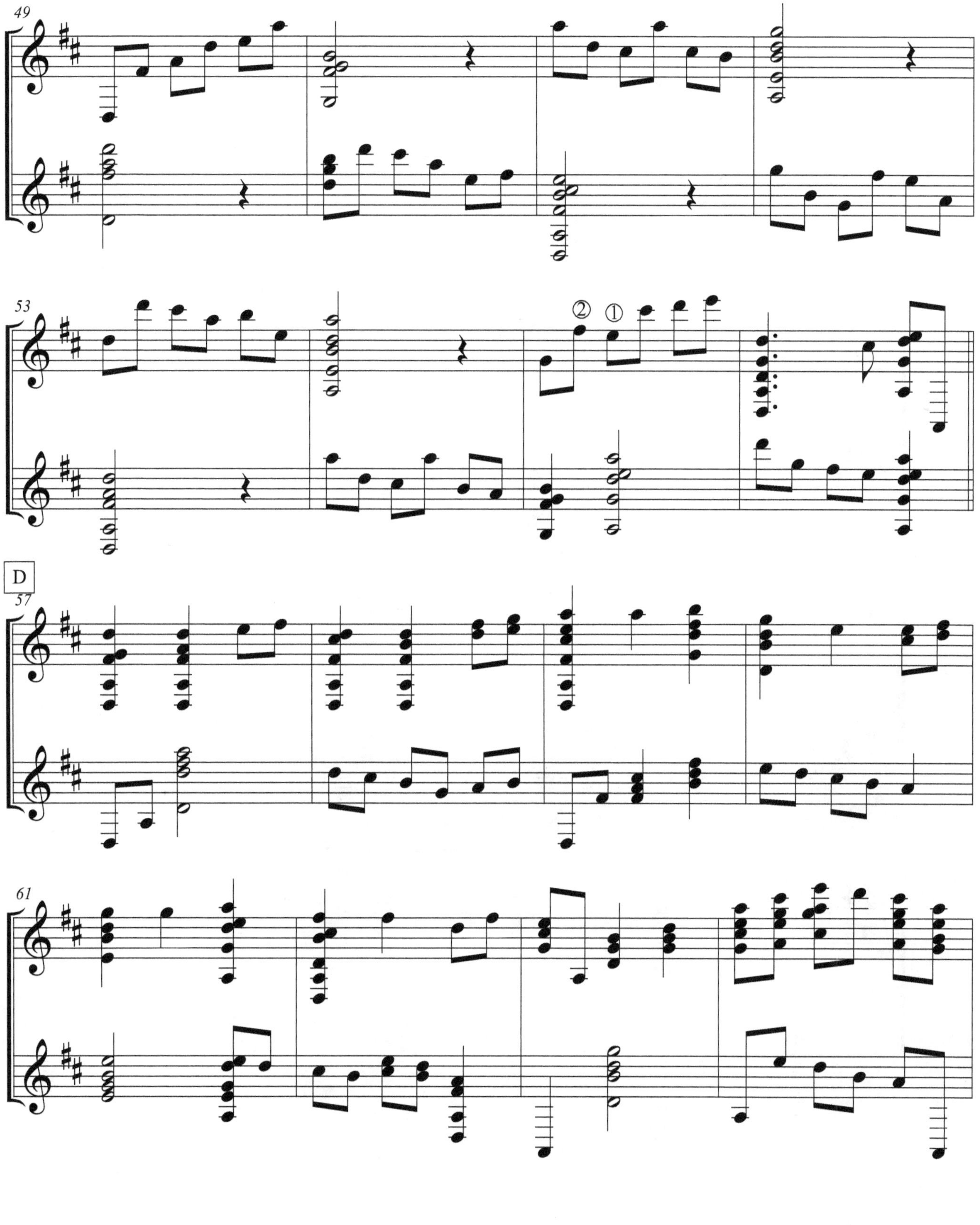
49
53
② ①
D
57
61

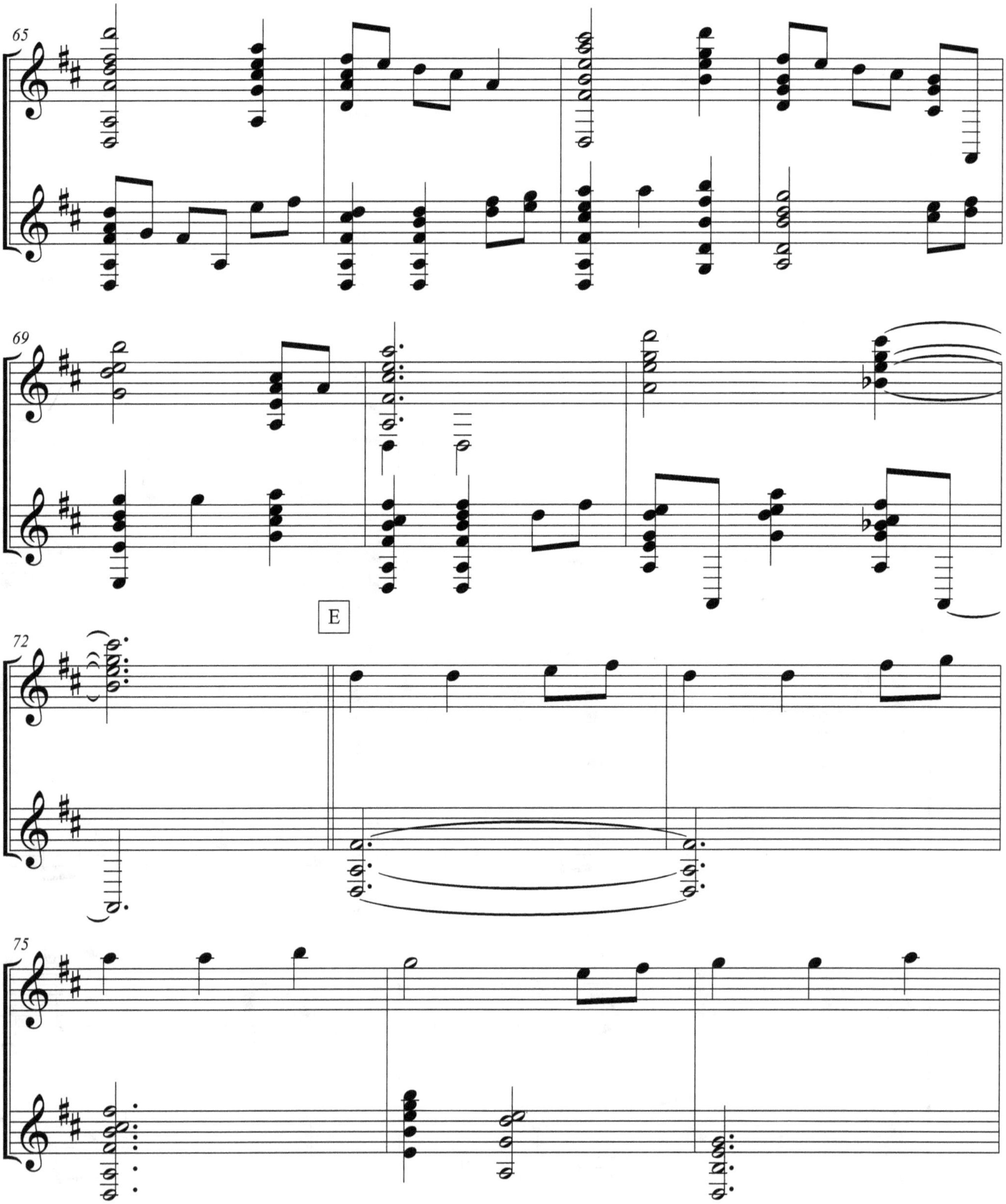
65
69
E
72
75

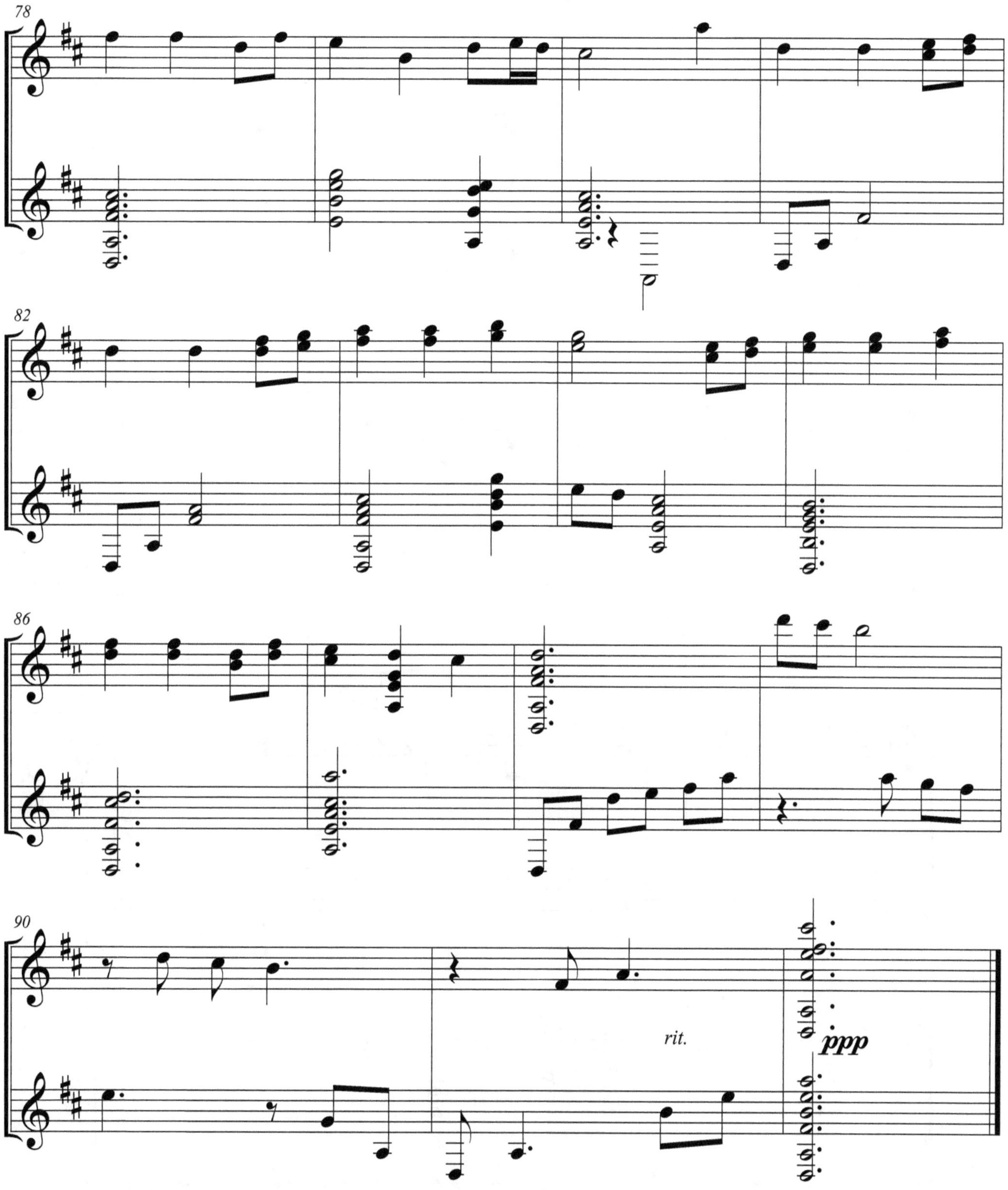
78
82
86
90
rit.
ppp

The Shepherd's Star

Dropped D Tuning

Early American Carol

William Bay

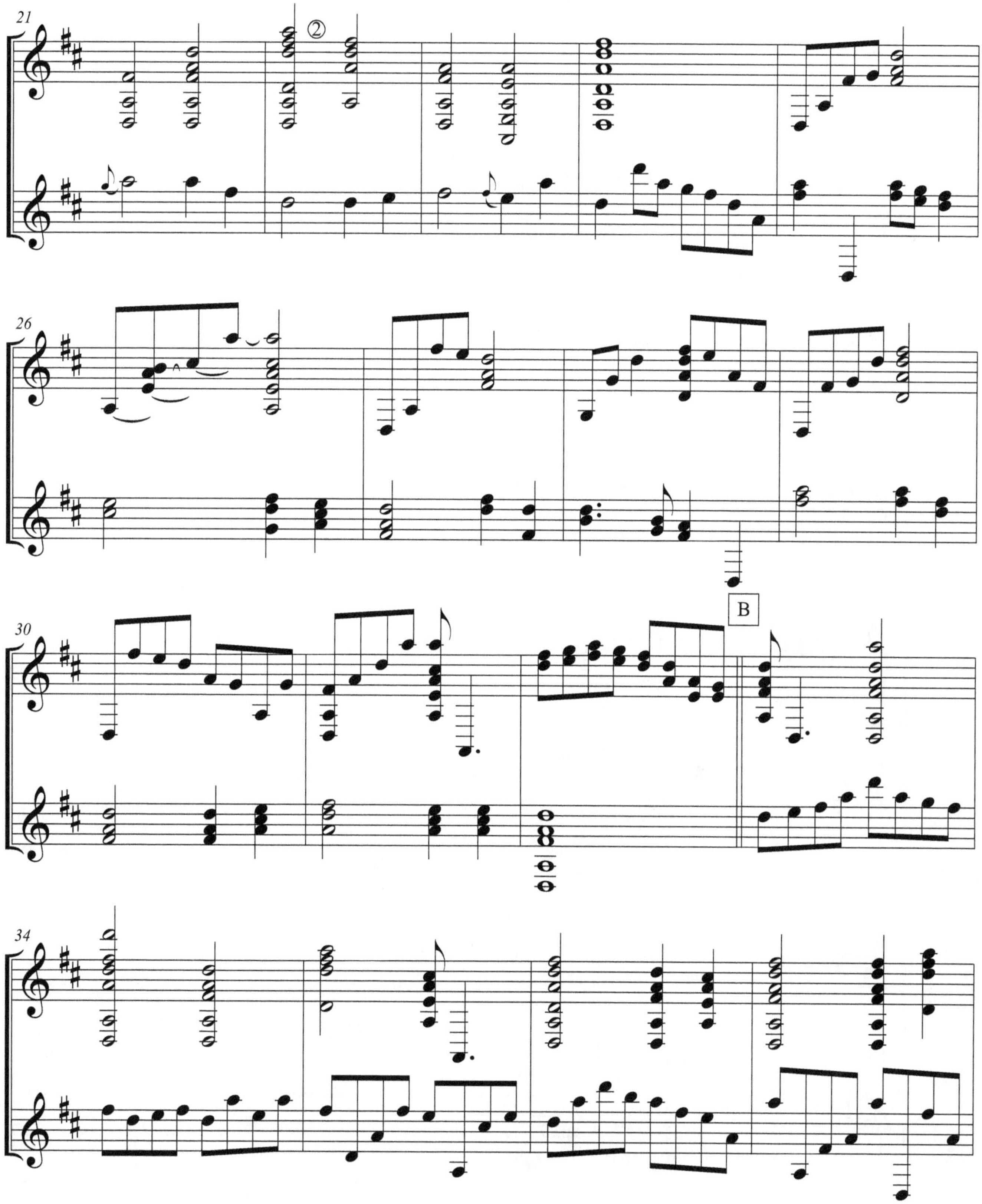
21
②
26
30
B
34

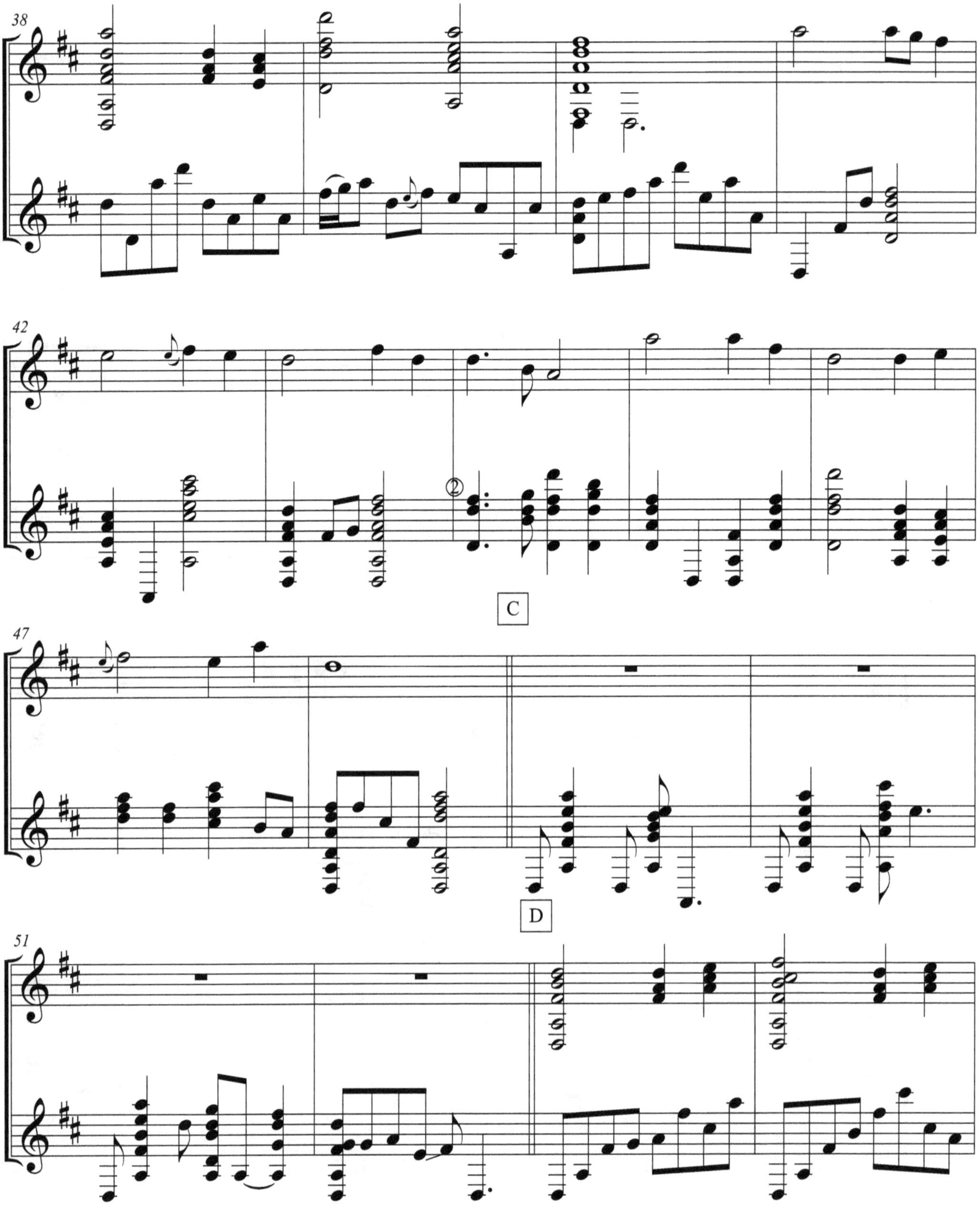
38
42
C
47
D
51

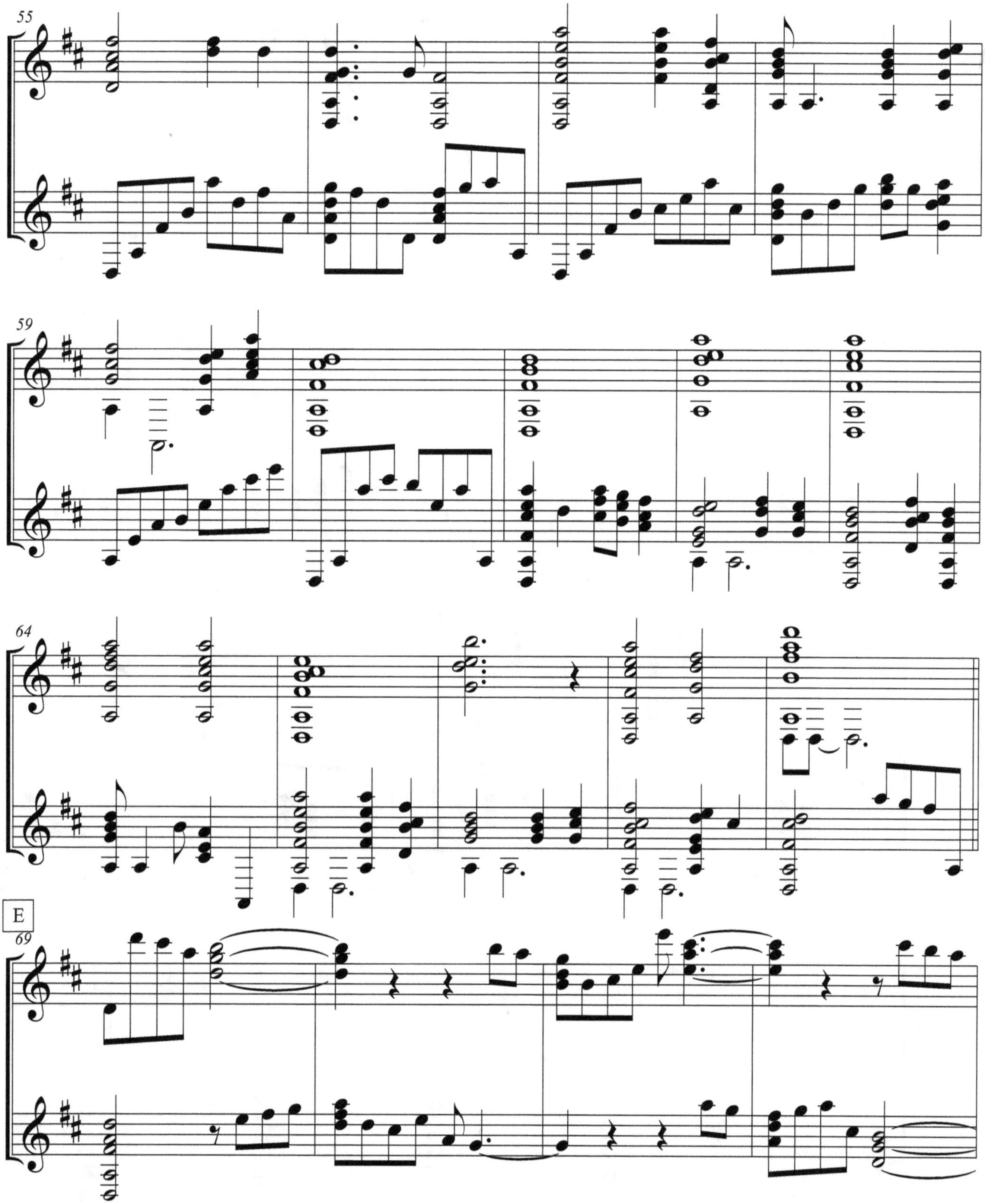
55
59
64
E
69

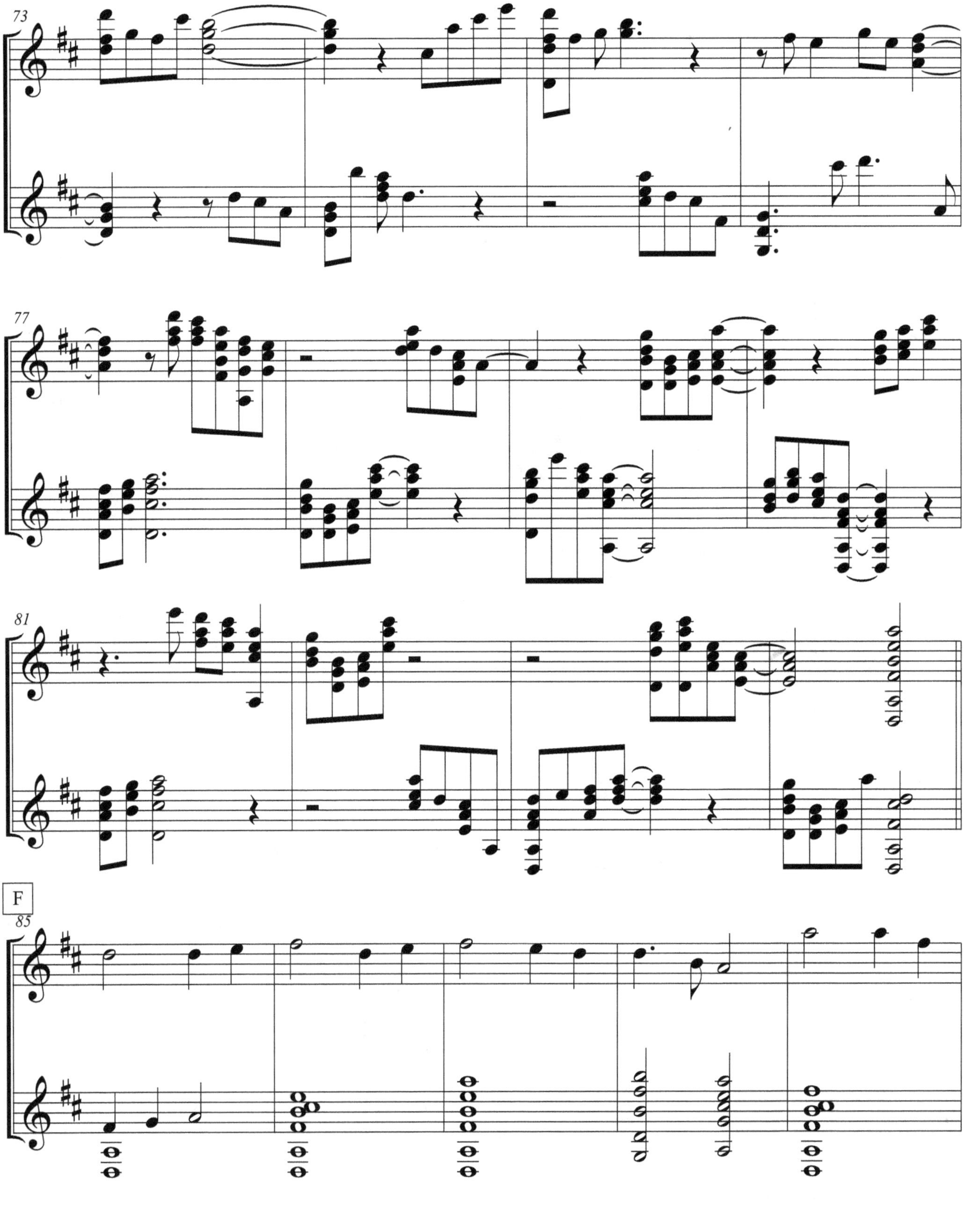
73
77
81
F
85

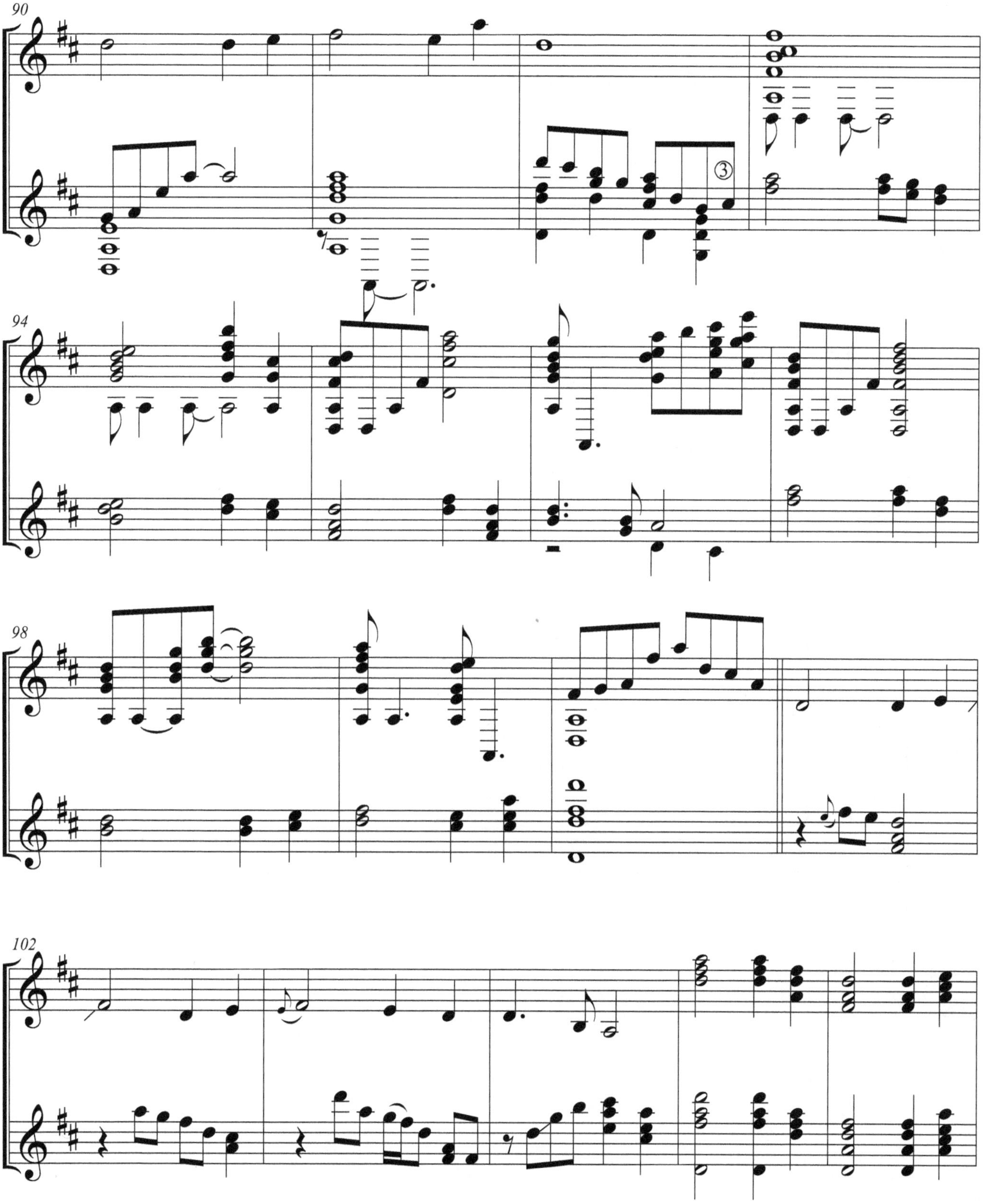
90
3
94
98
102

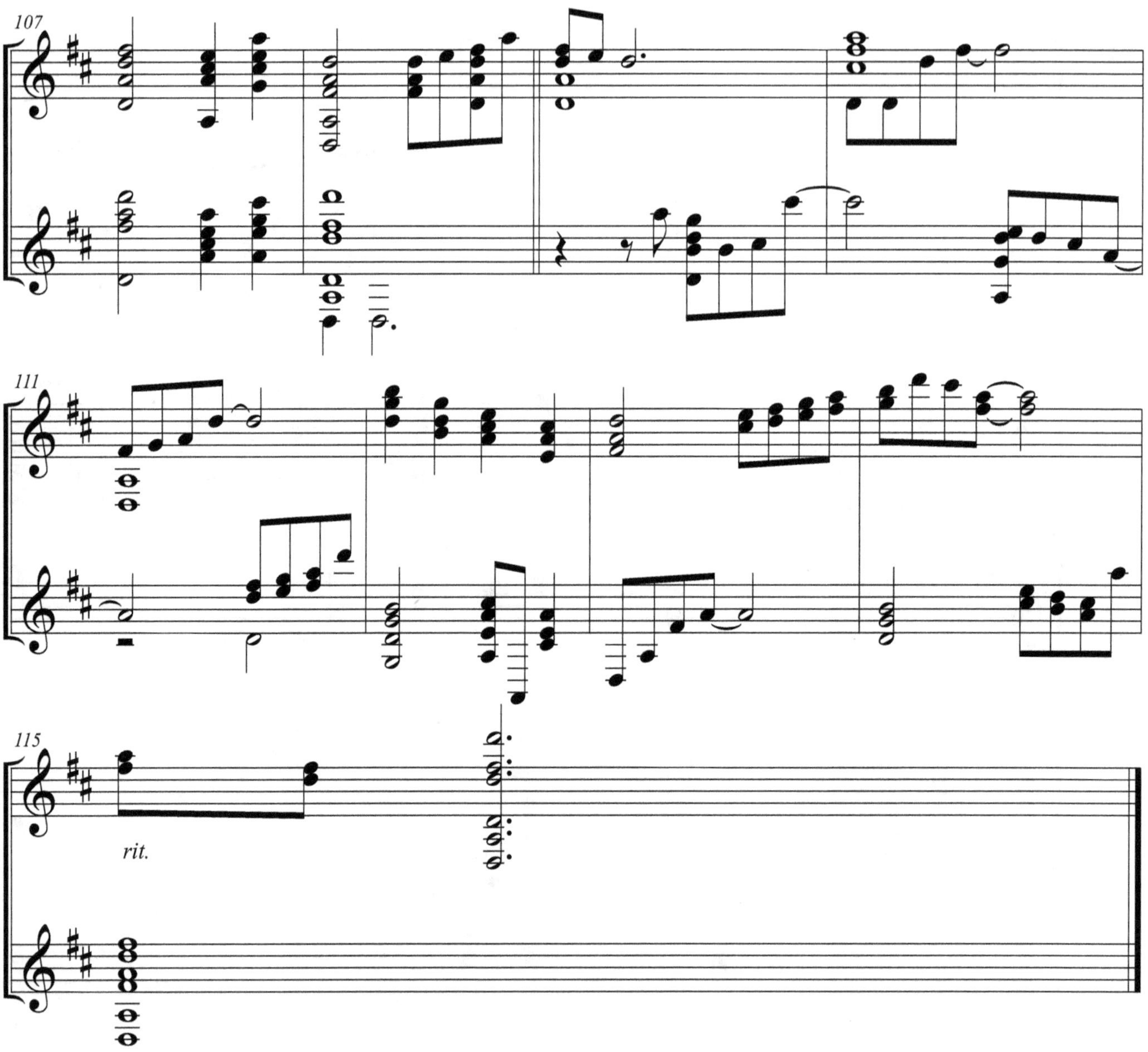
107
111
115
rit.

Baloo, Lammy; The First Noel; Silent Night

Dropped D Tuning

17th Century Scottish Carol

William Bay

E The First Noel

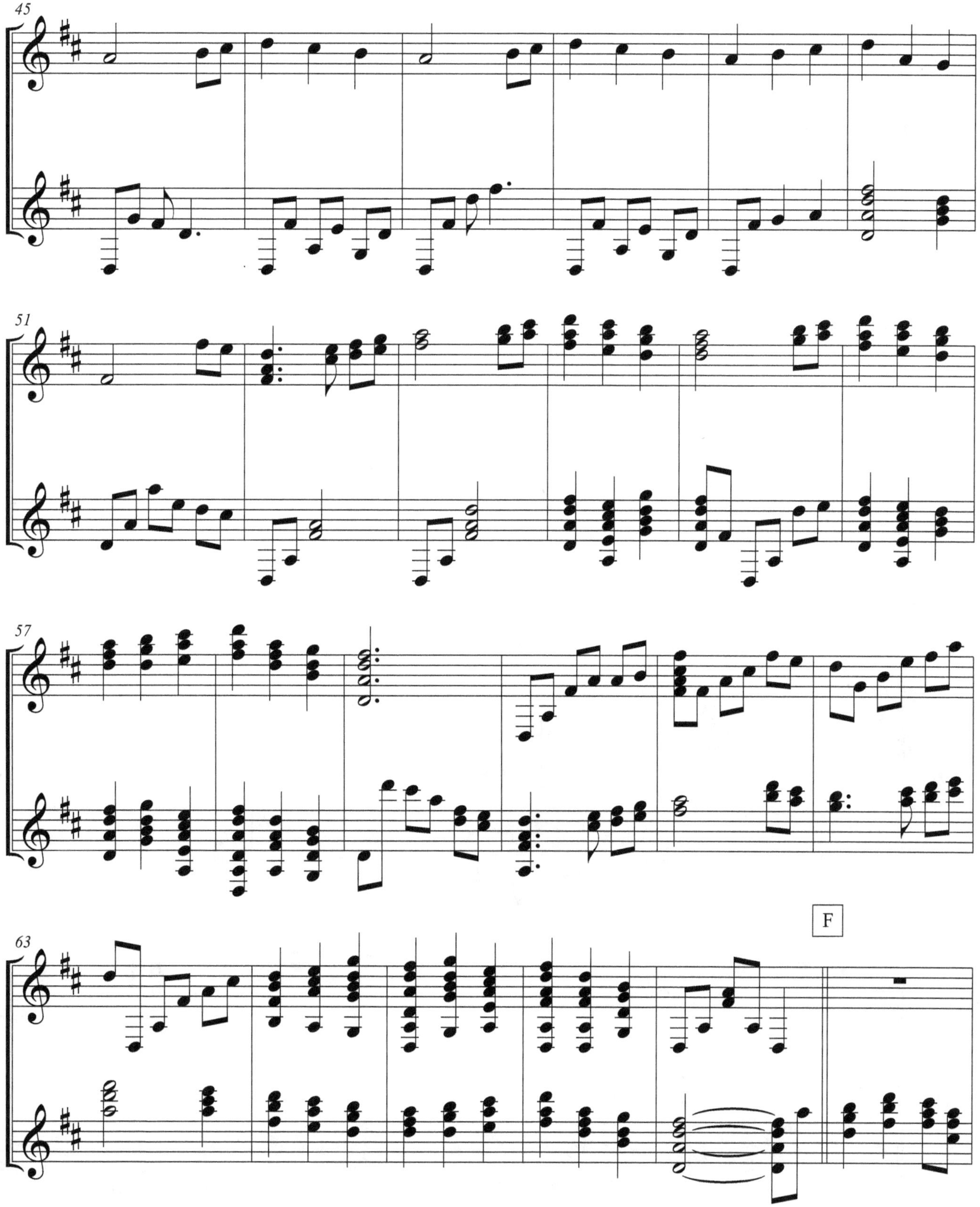
45
51
57
63
F

G Silent Night

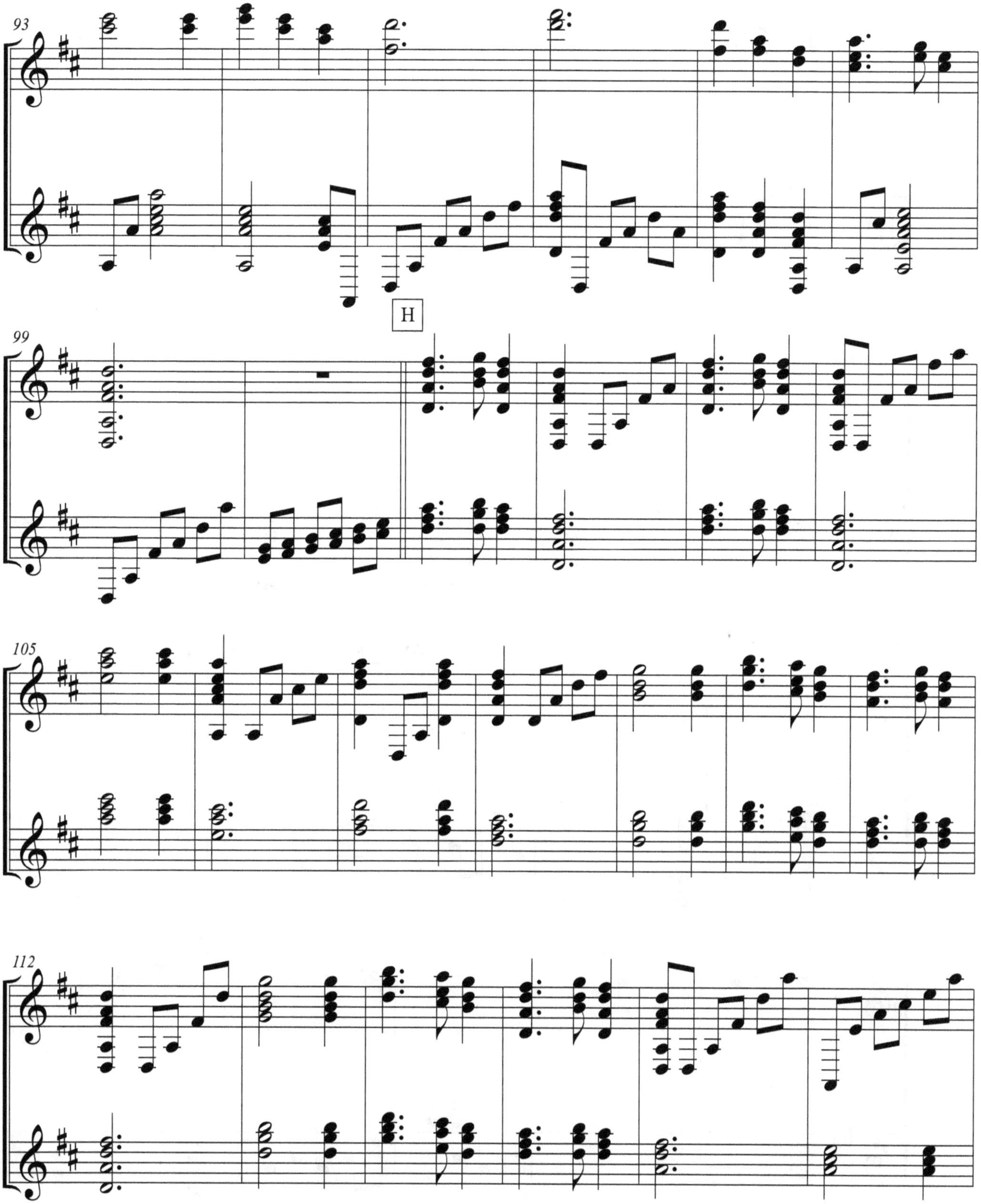
93
H
99
105
112

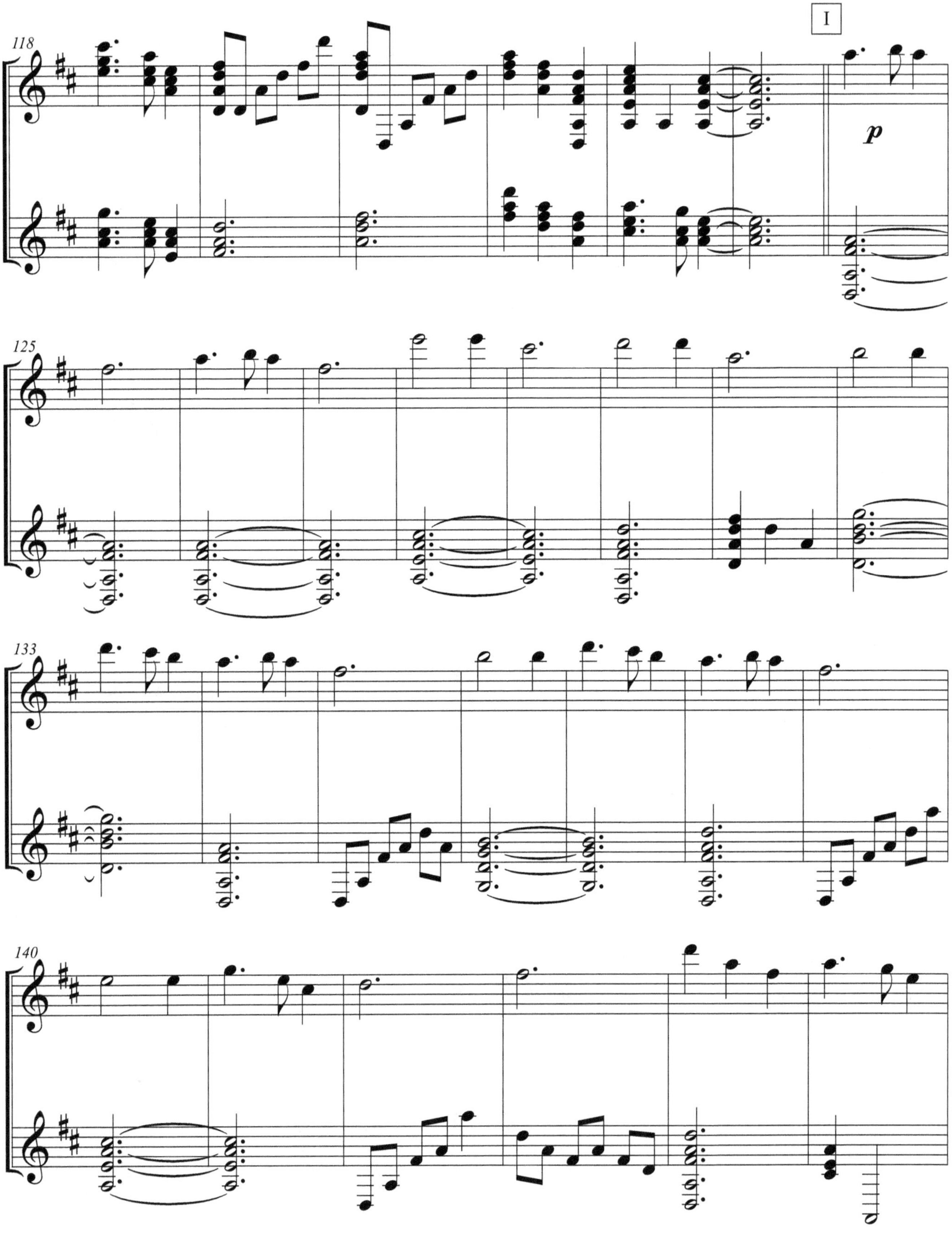
118
I
p
125
133
140

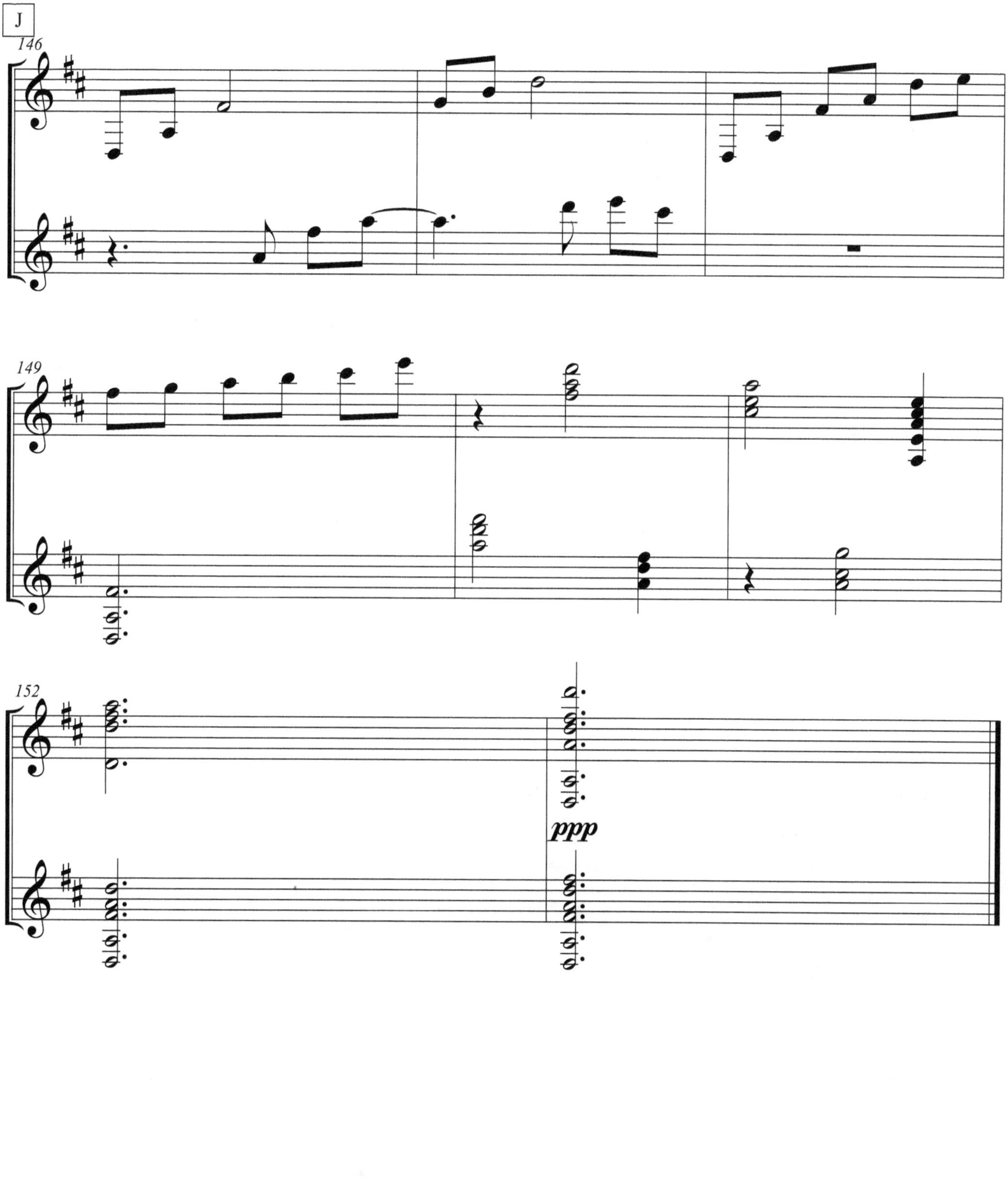
J
146
149
152
ppp

Christmas Prayer

Dropped D Tuning

William Bay

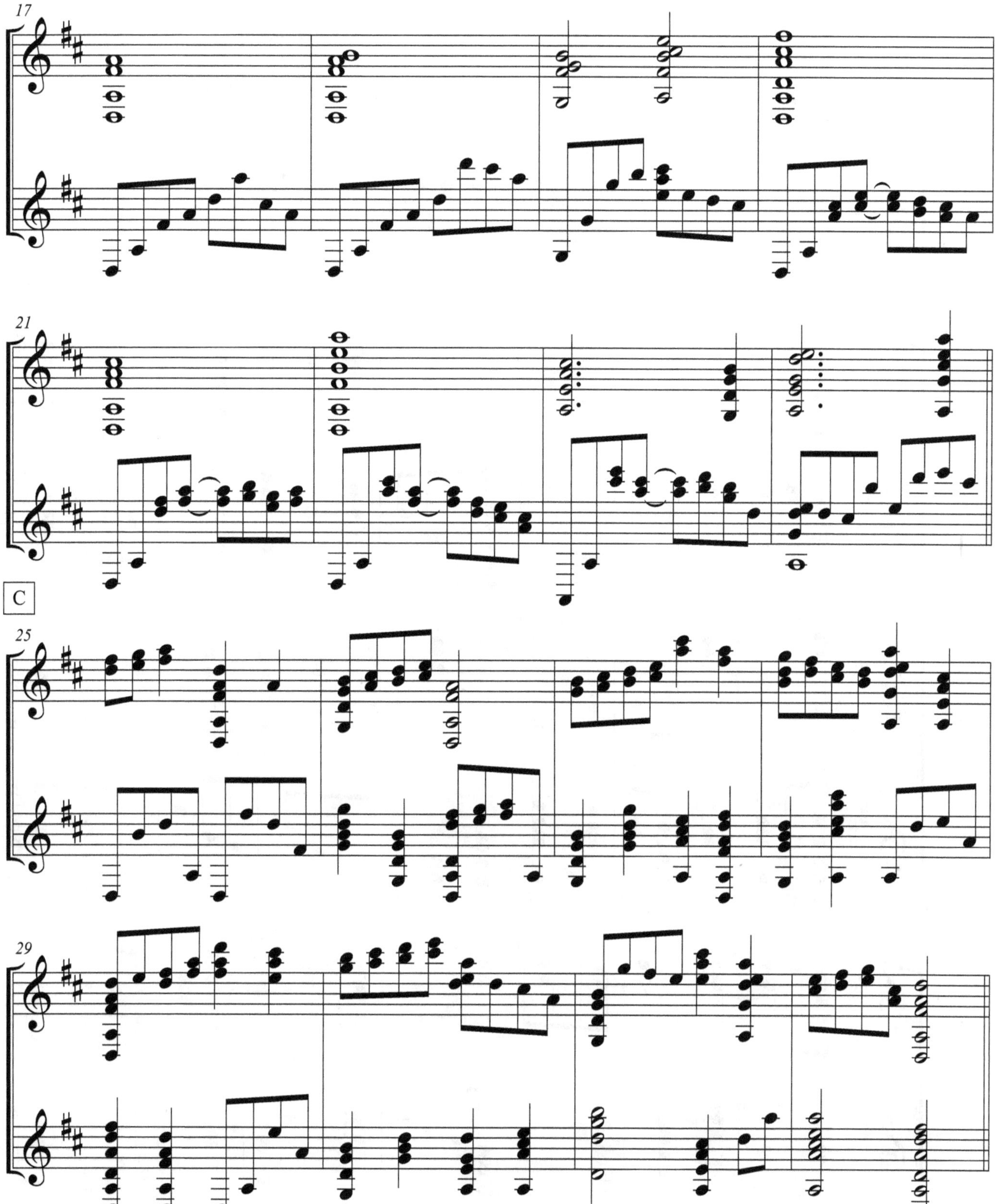
17
21
C
25
29

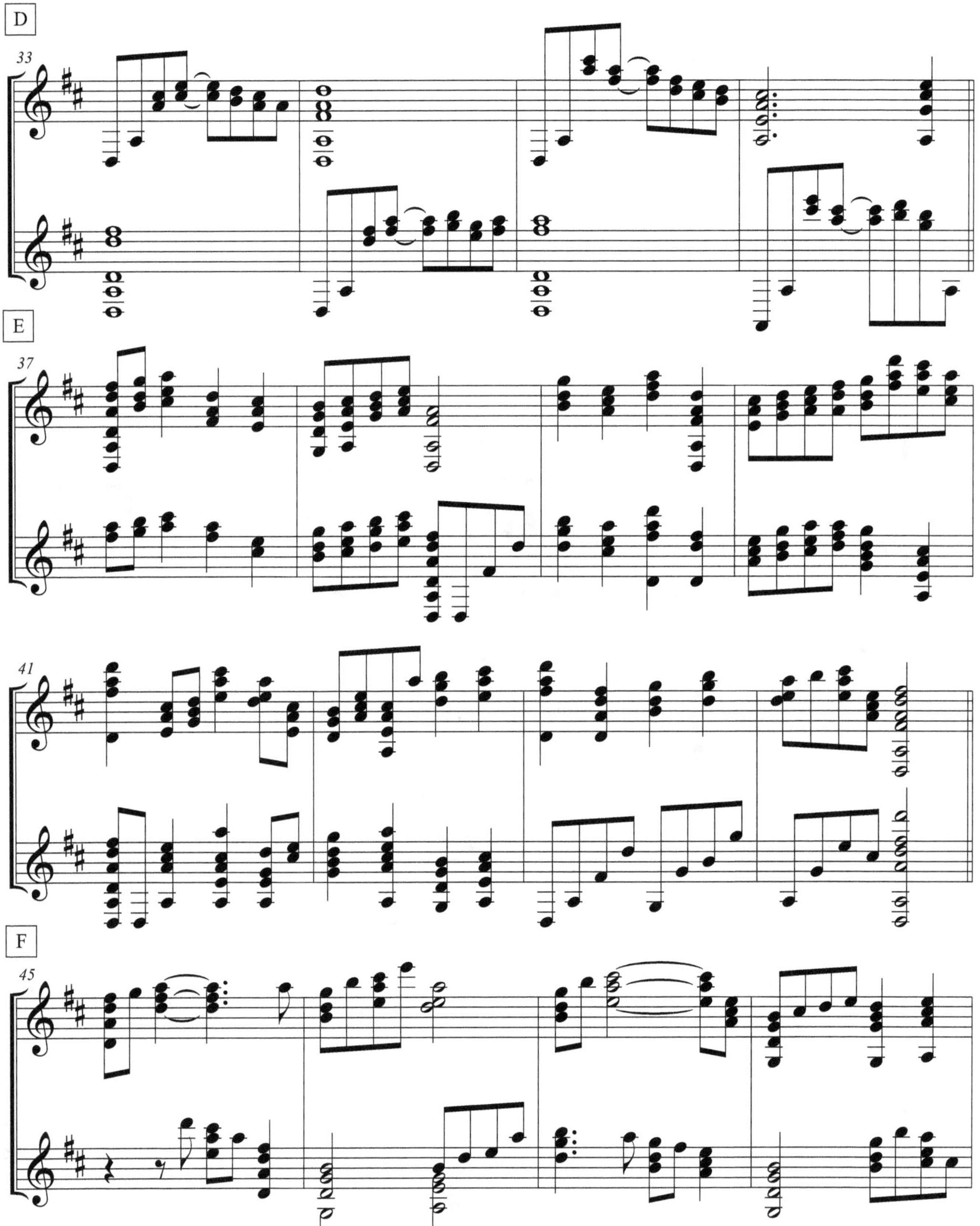
D
33
E
37
41
F
45

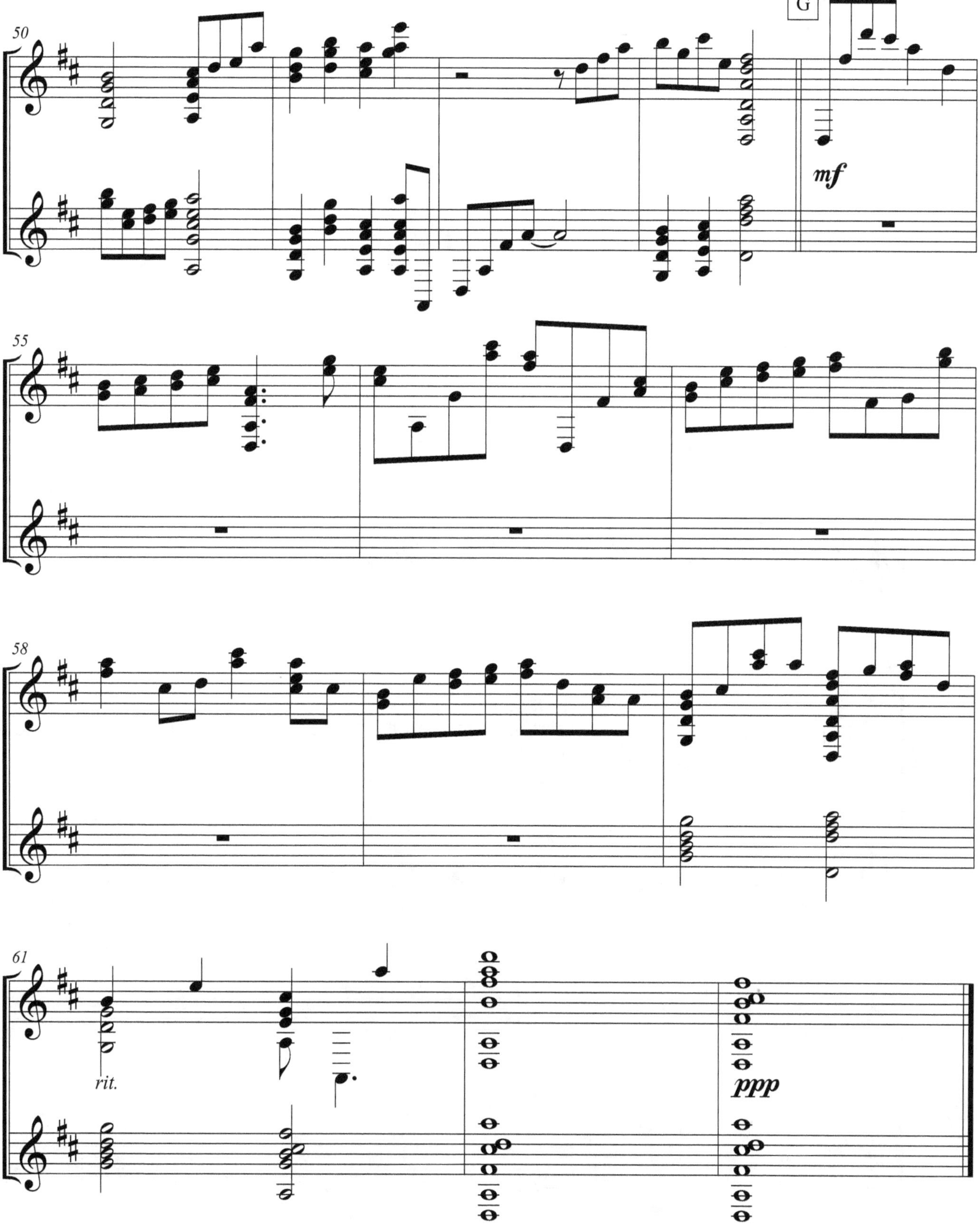
50
G
mf
55
58
61
rit.
ppp

A Virgin Unspotted

Dropped D Tuning

Early American Carol

William Bay

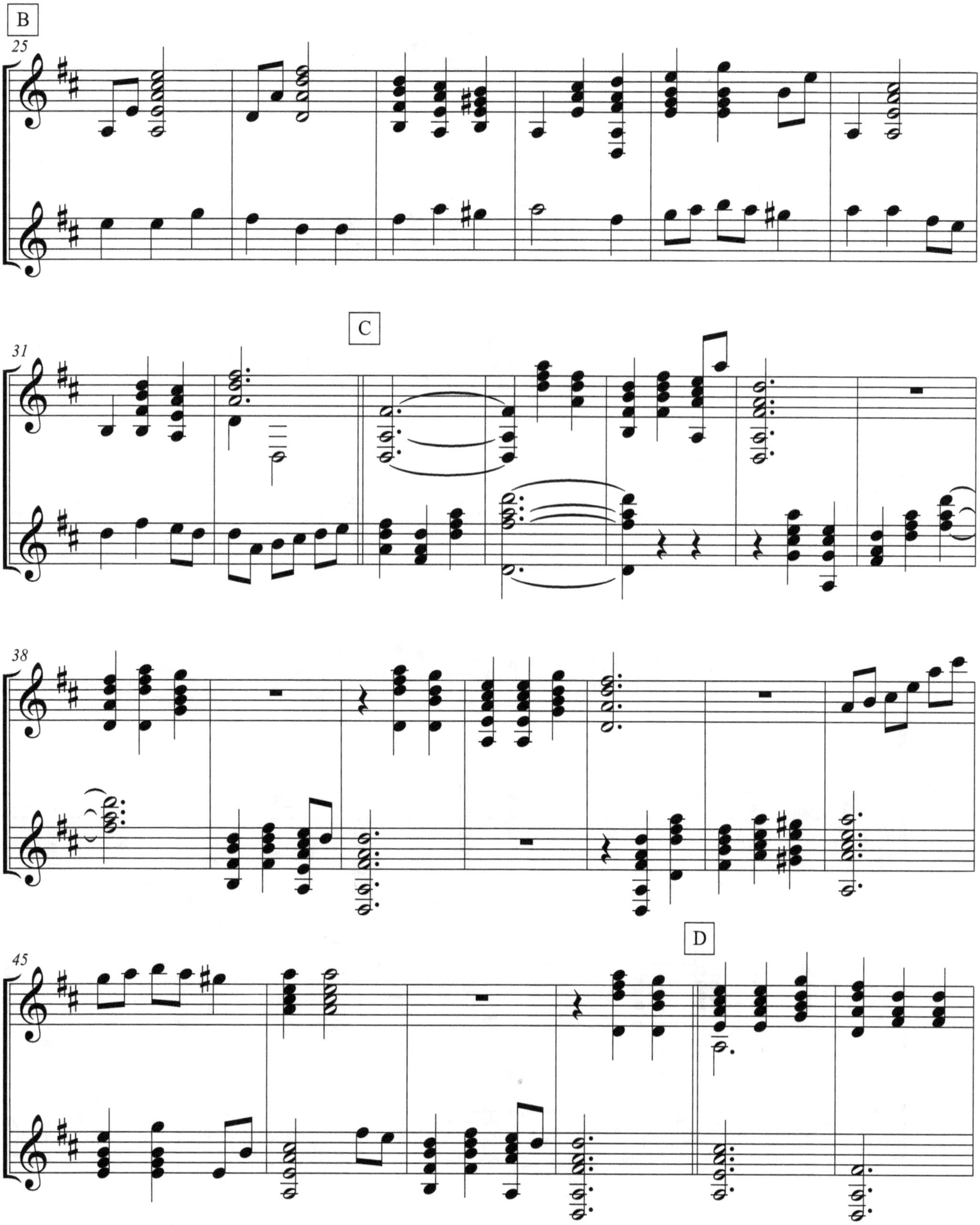
B
25
C
31
38
45
D

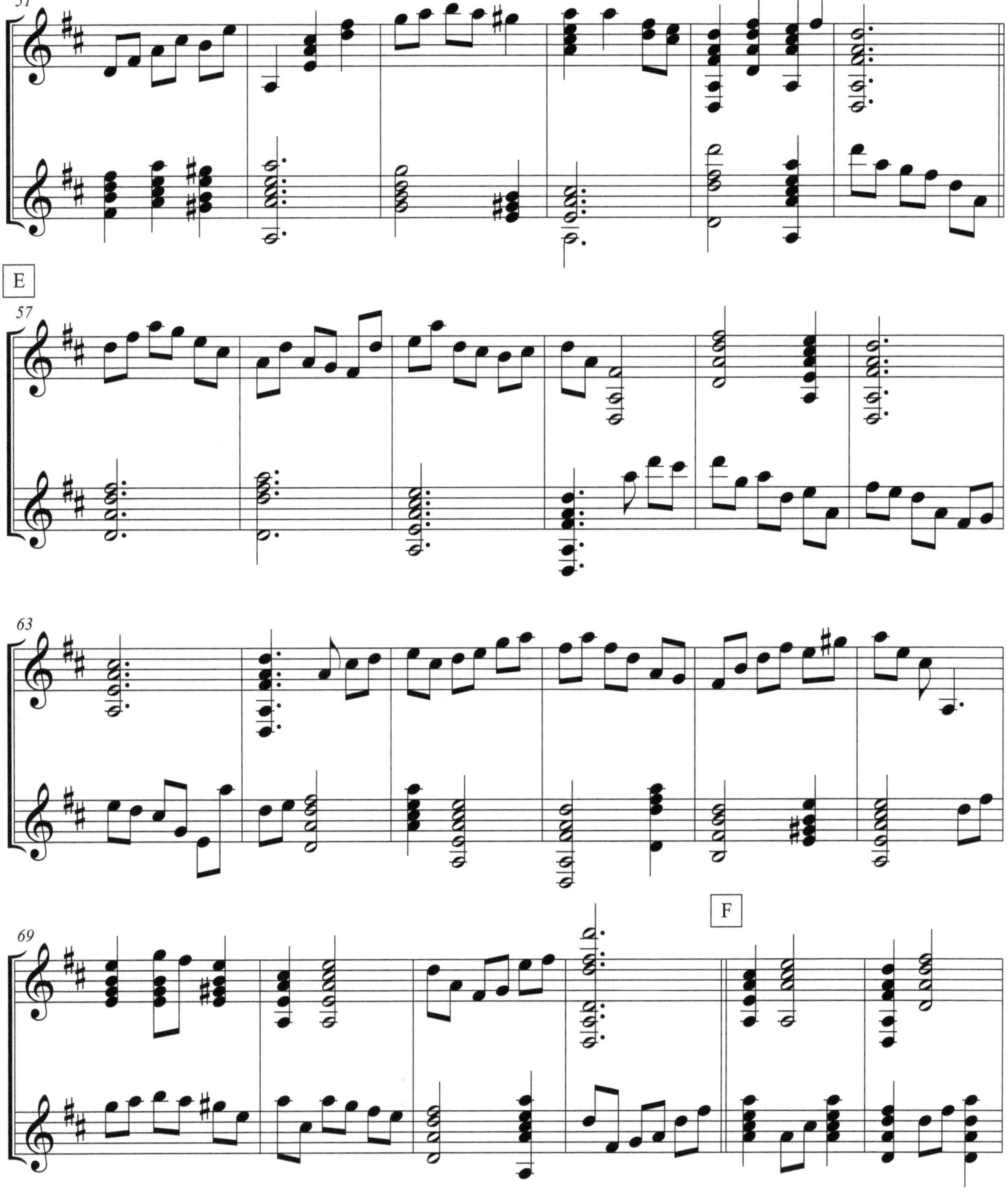
51
E
57
63
F
69

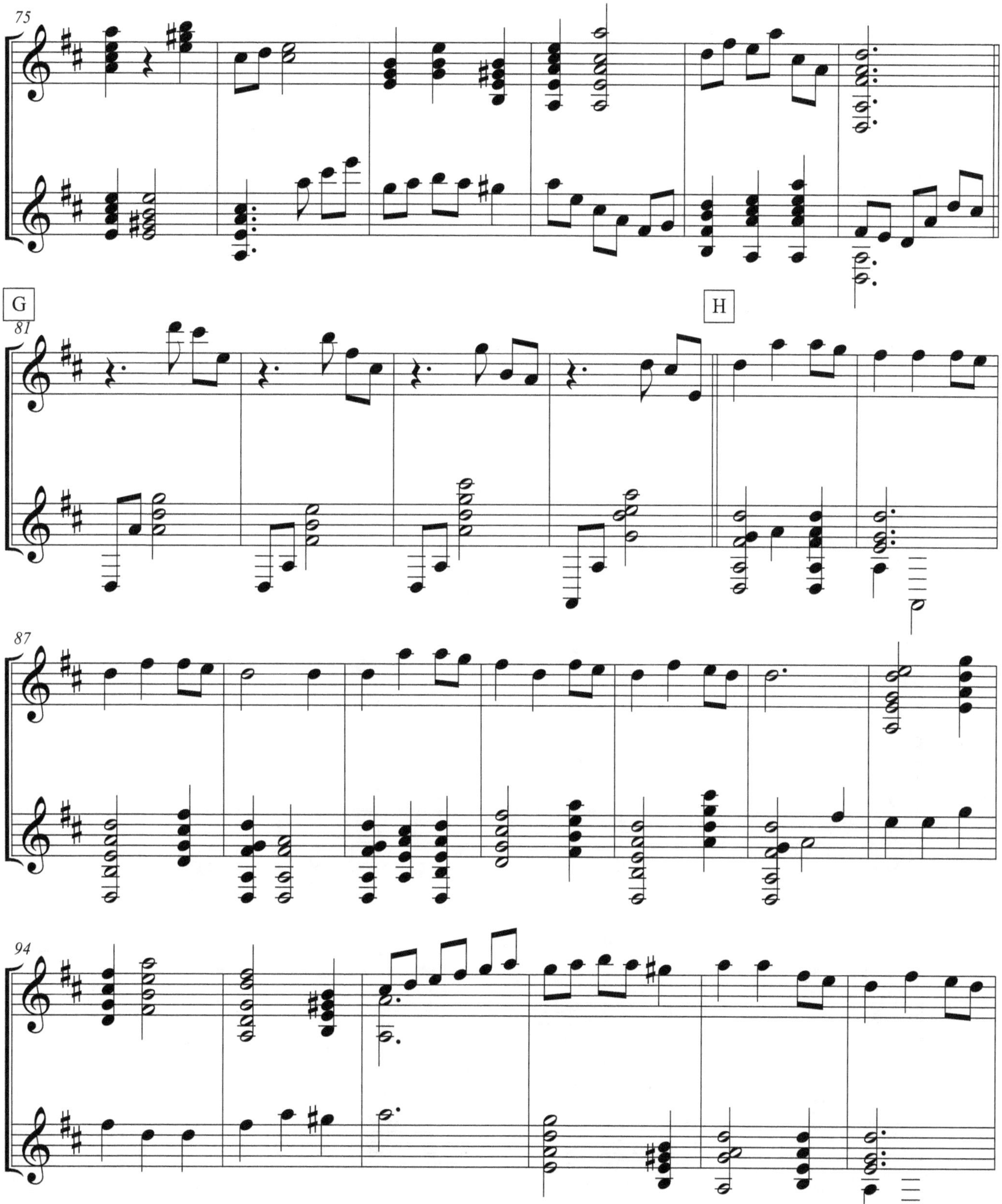
75
G
81
H
87
94

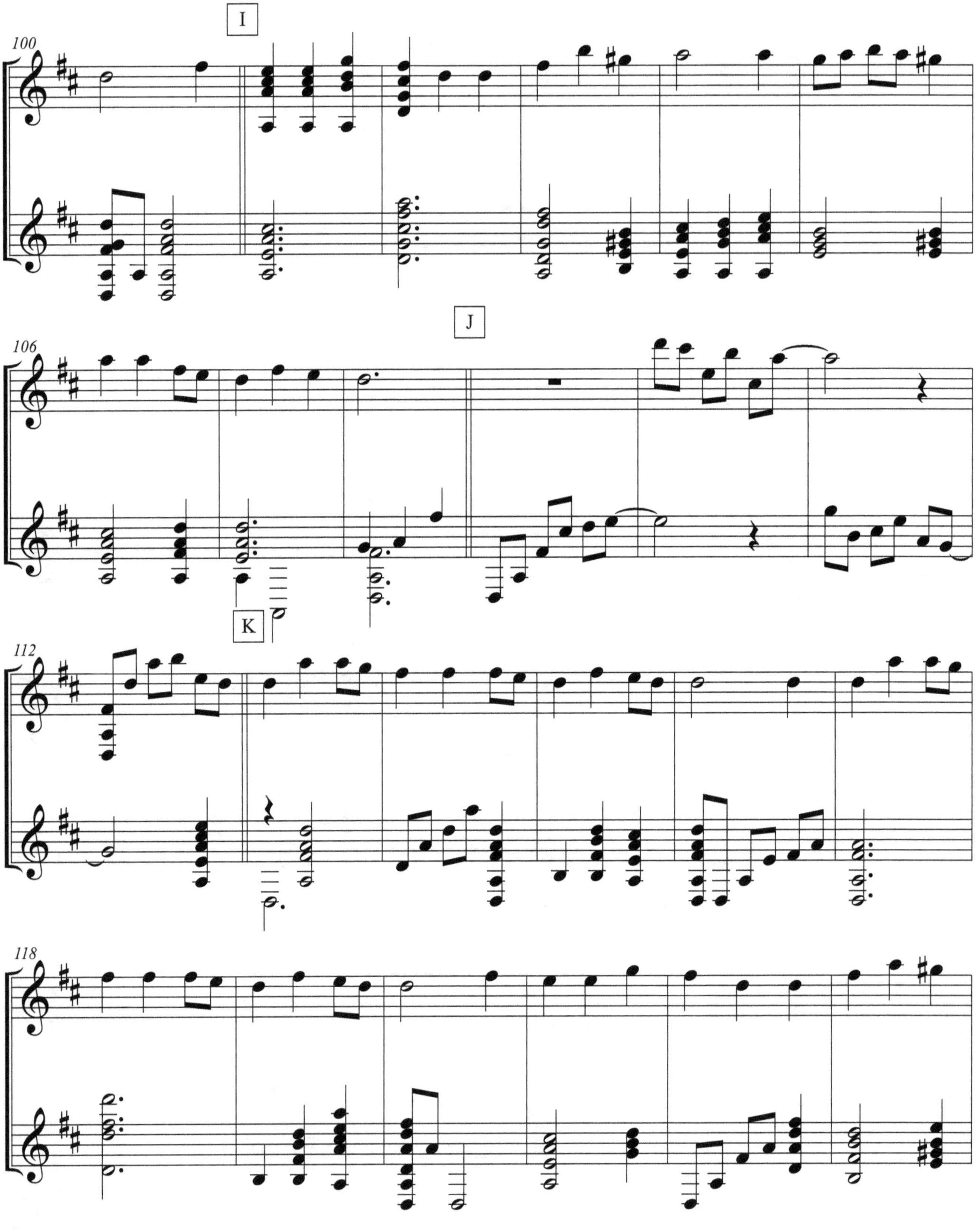
100
I
106
J
112
K
118

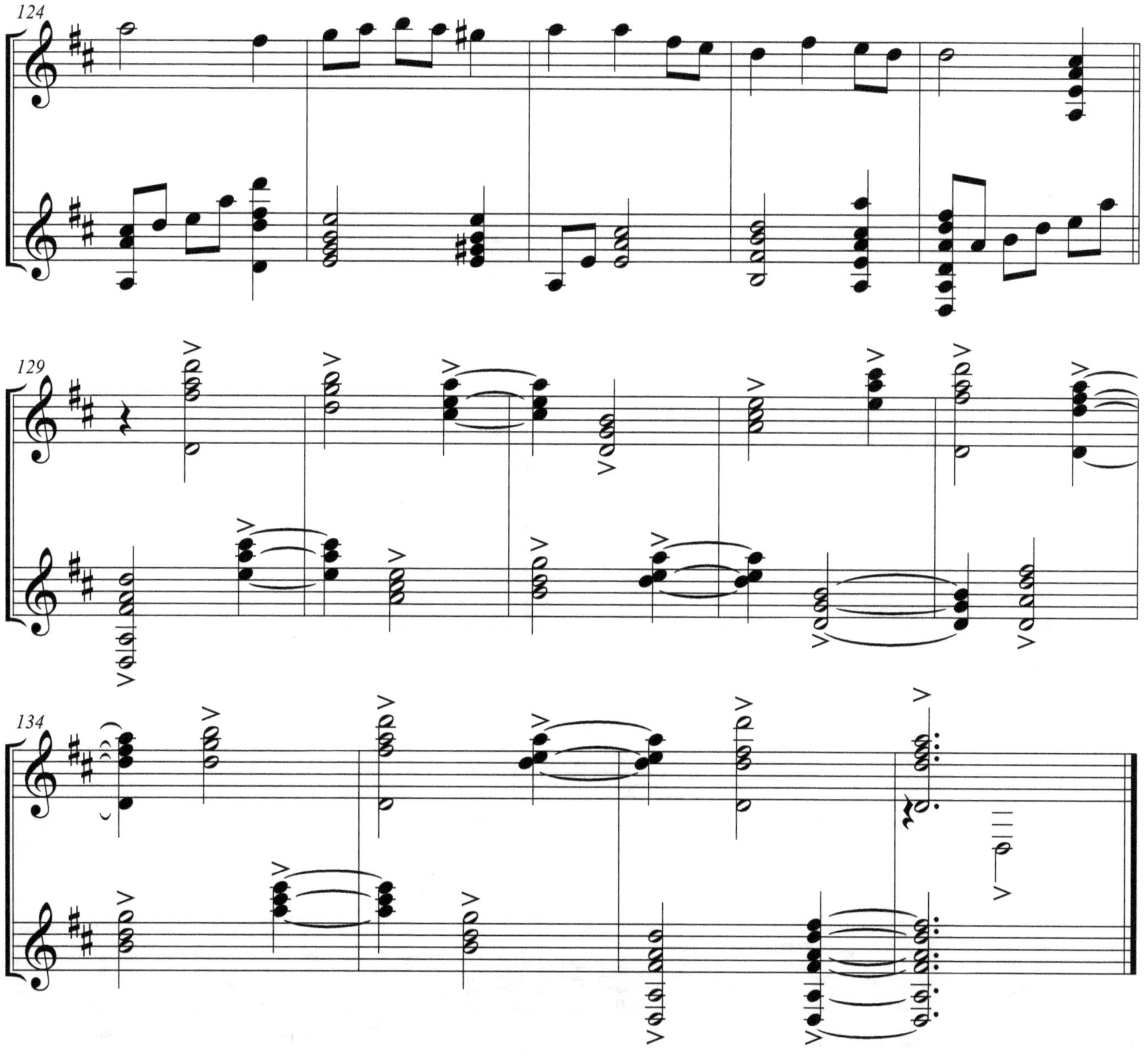
124
129
134

Green Grow'th The Holly

16th Century England

William Bay

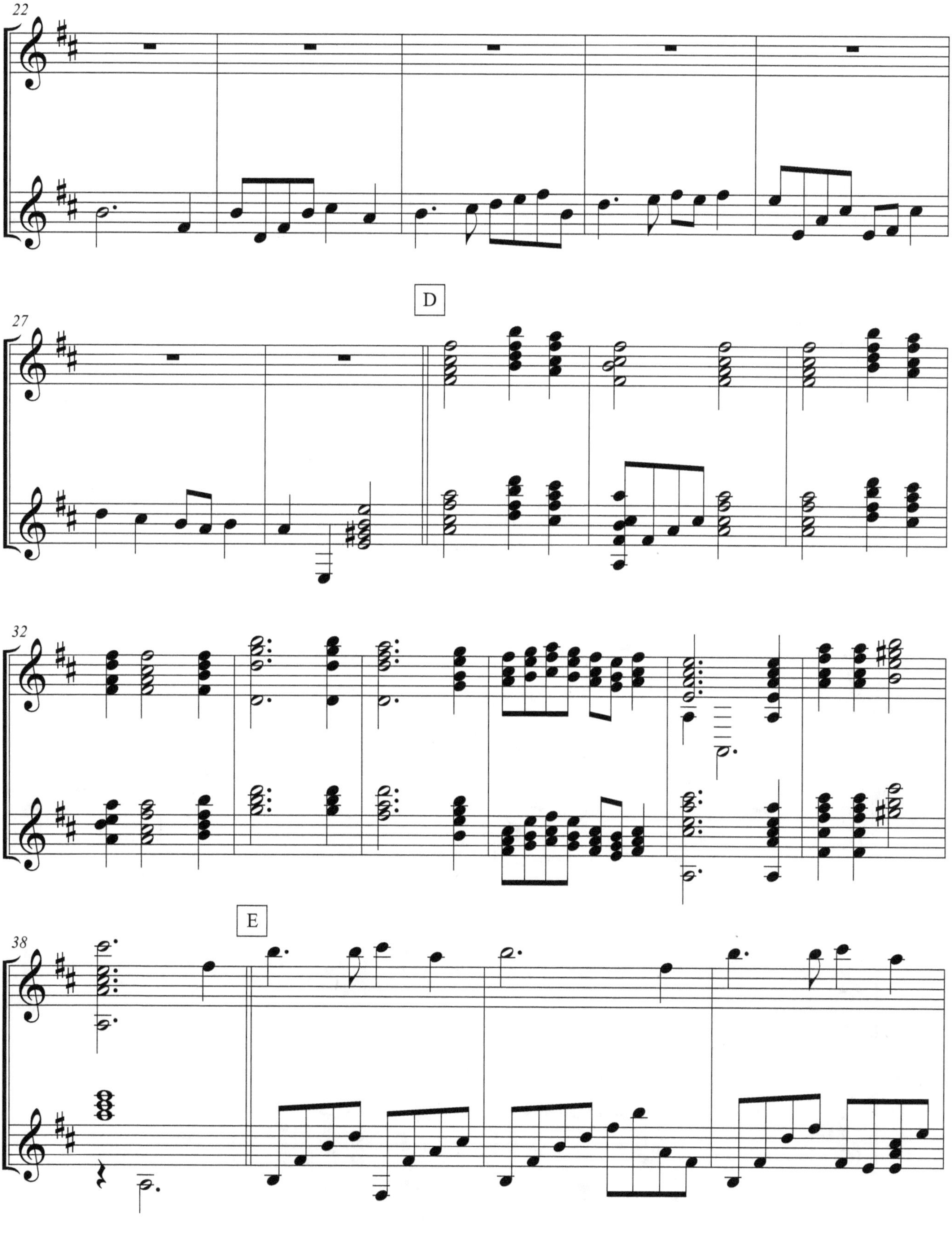
22
27
D
32
38
E

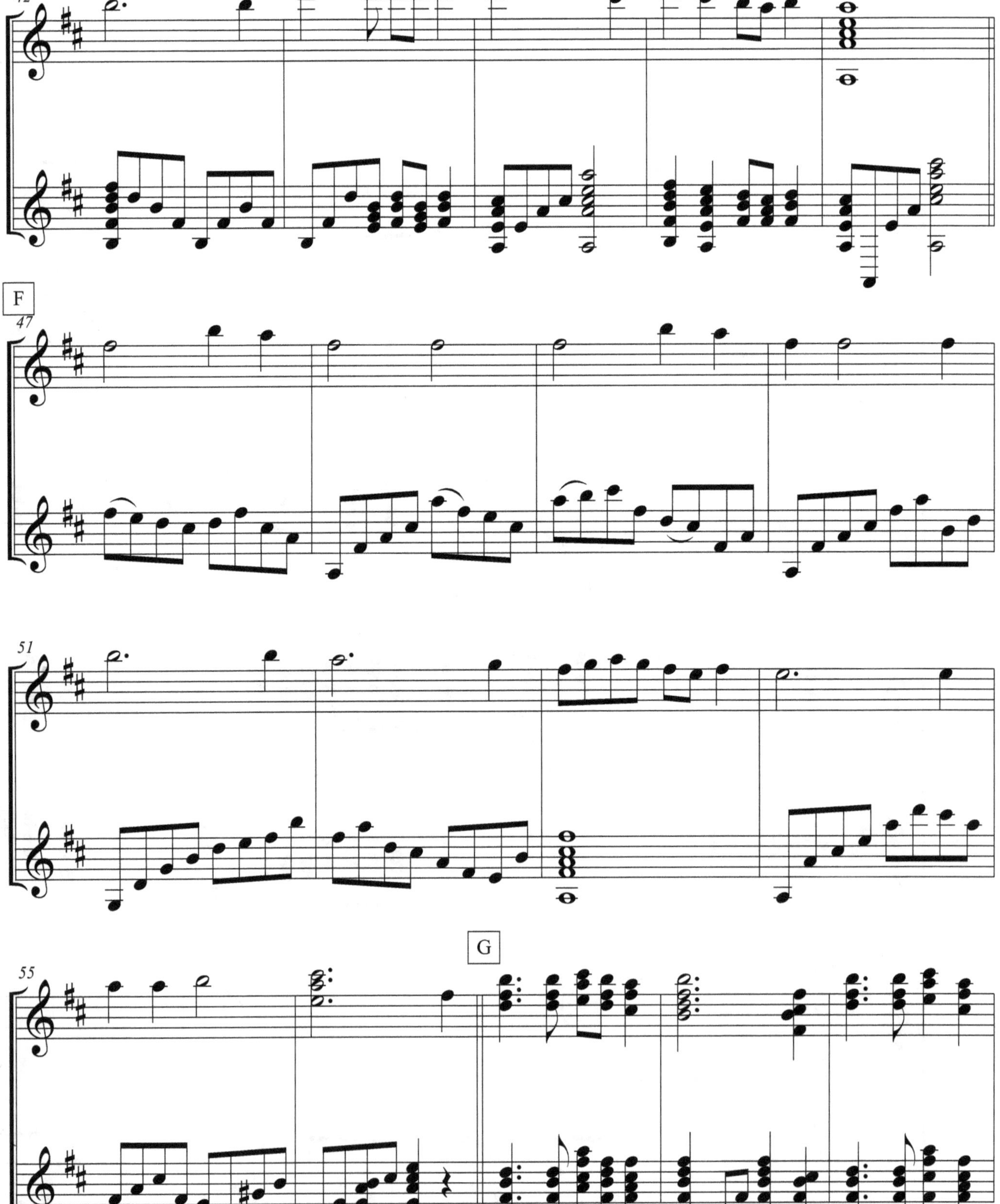
42
F
47
51
G
55

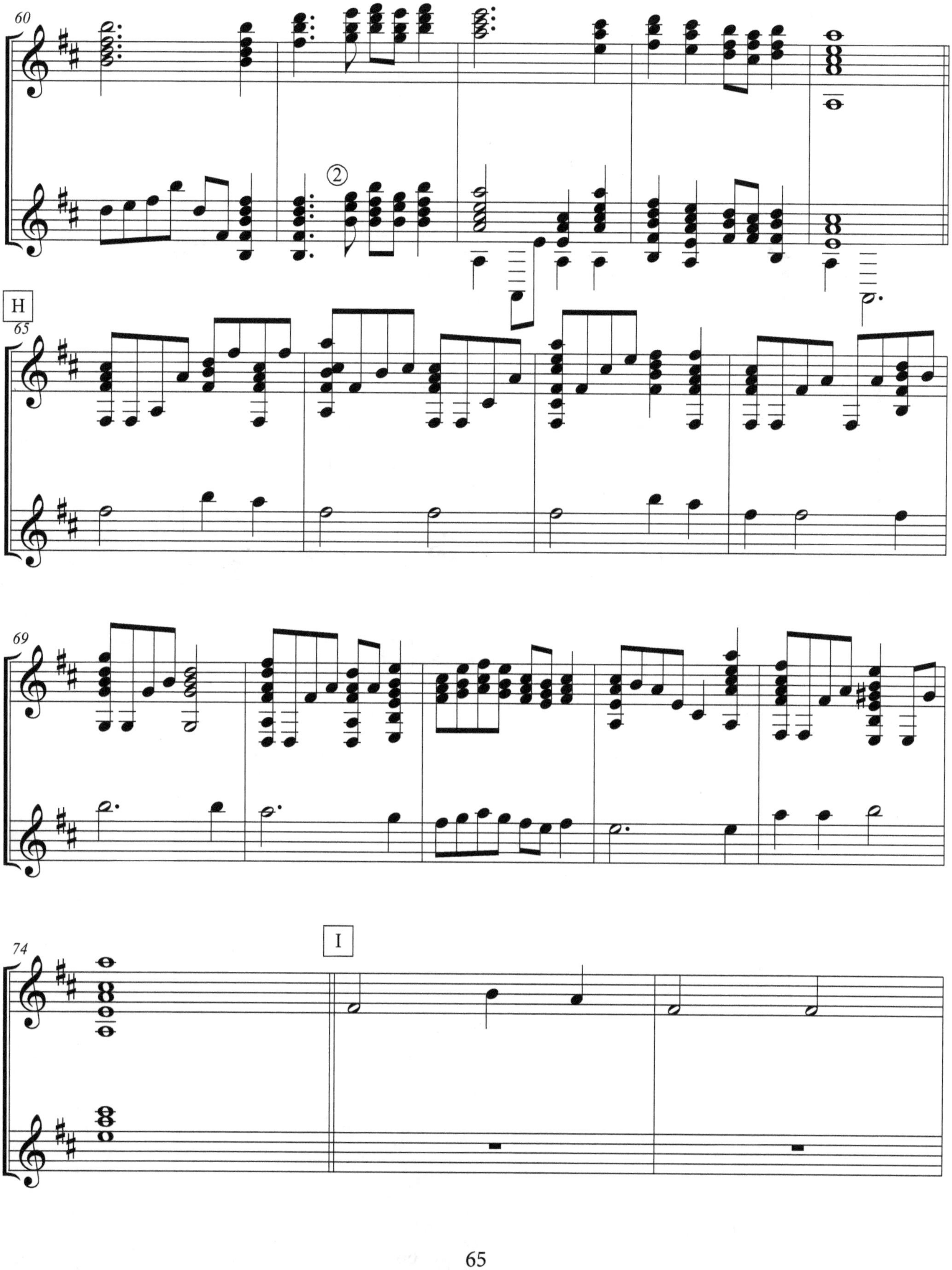
60
②
H
65
69
74
I

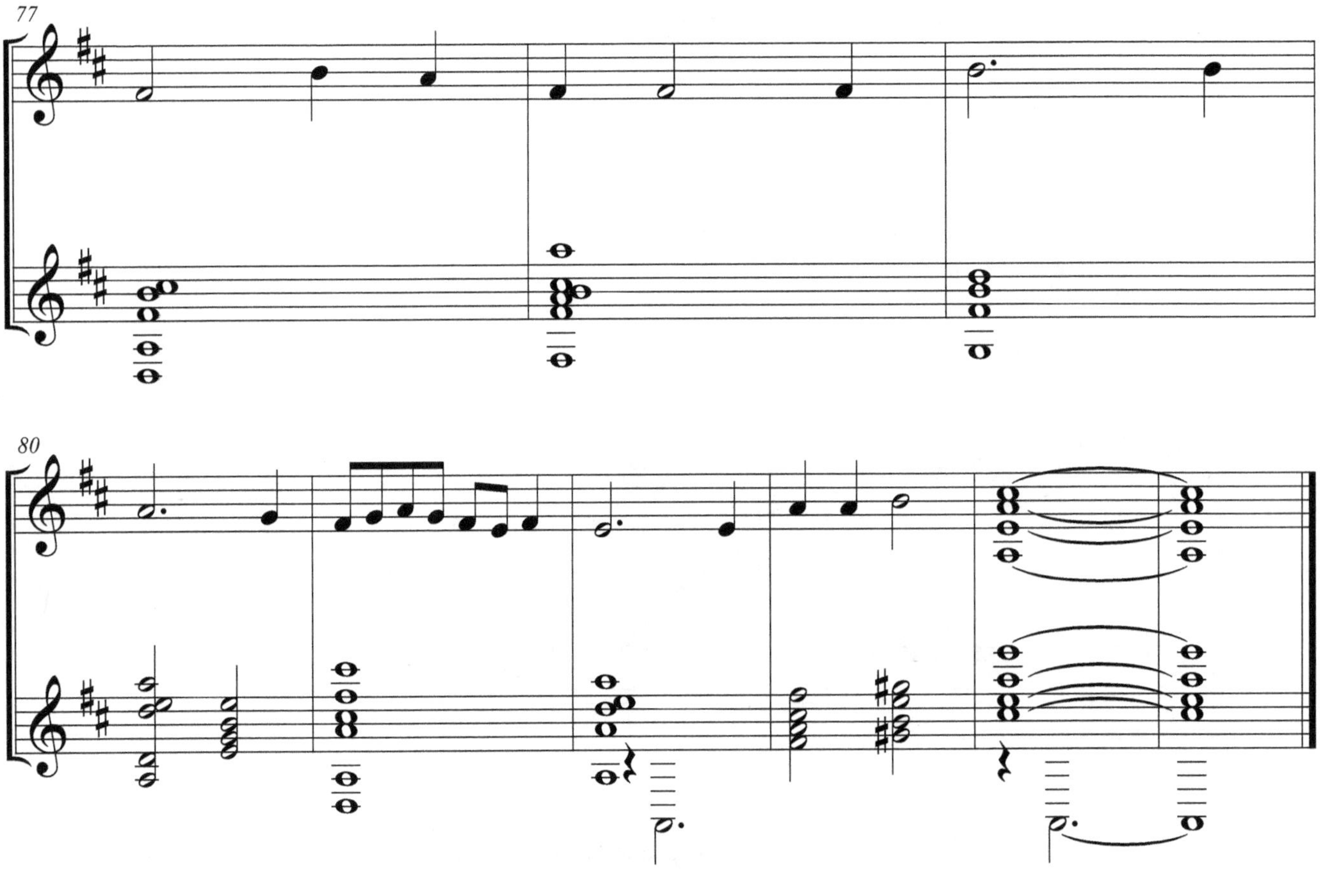
77
80

This page has been left blank
to avoid awkward page turns.

What Child Is This

Rhythmically ♩. = 62

Arranged by William Bay

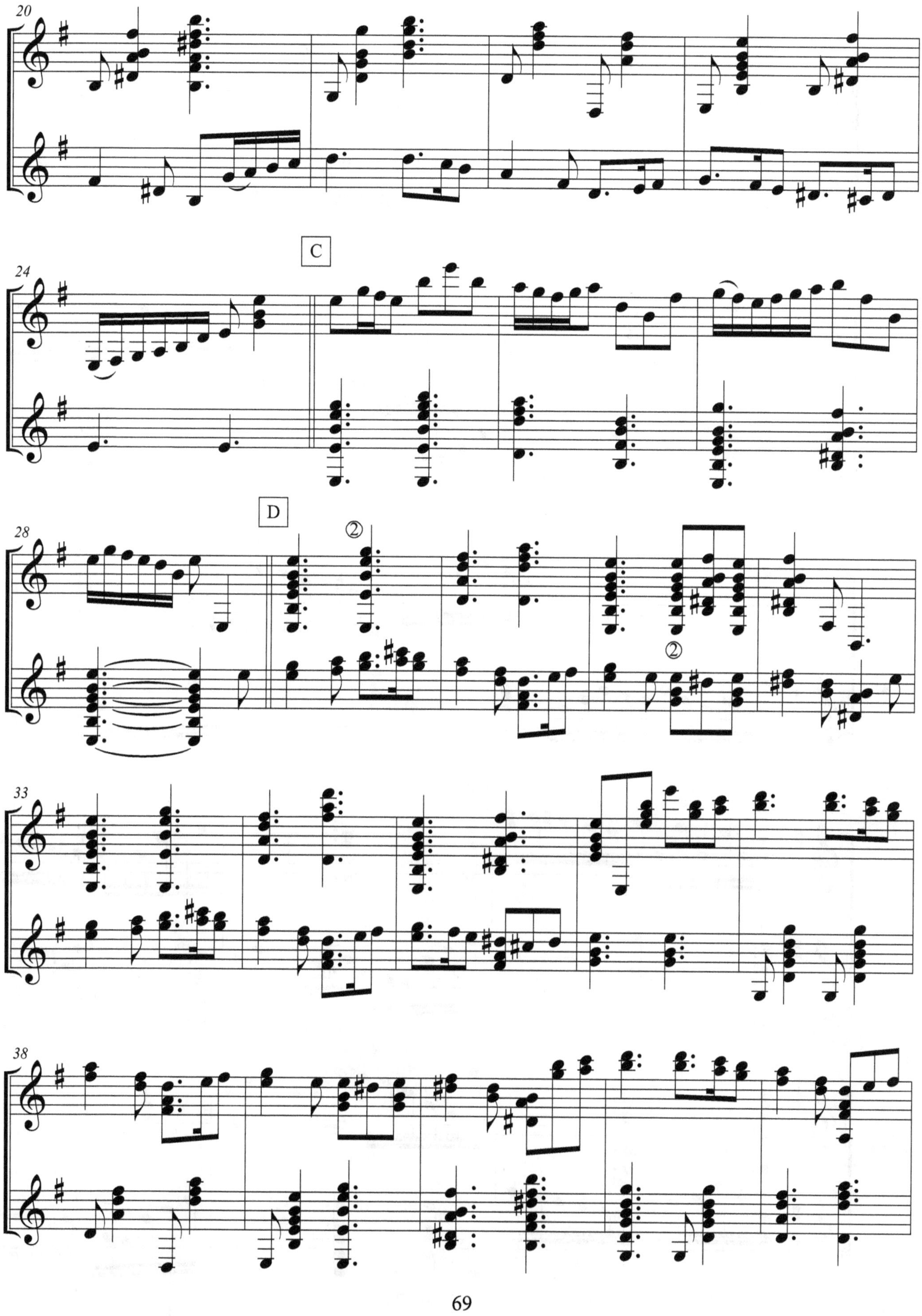
20
24
C
28
D
33
38

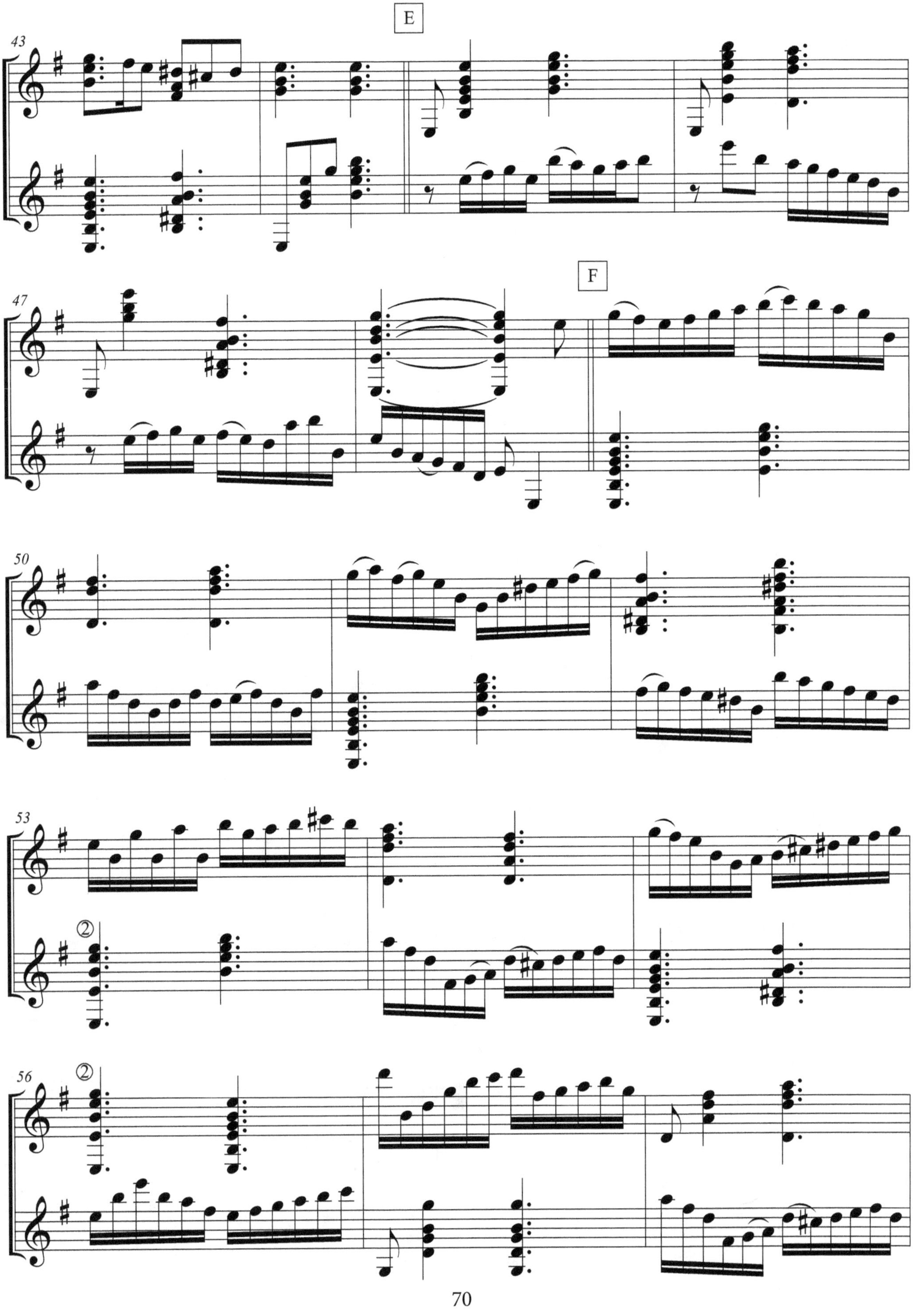
E
43
F
47
50
53
②
56
②

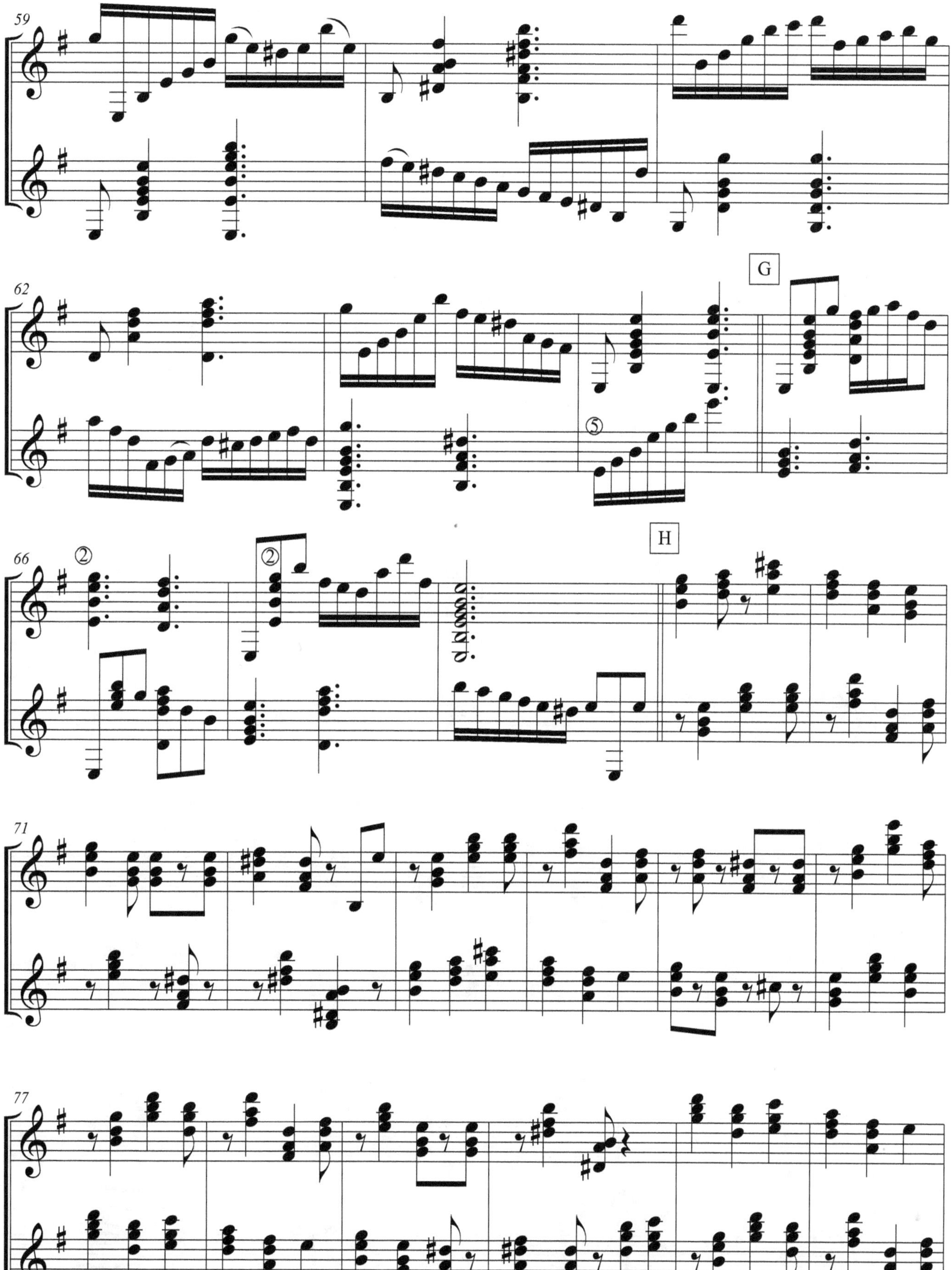
59
62
⑤
G
66
②
②
H
71
77

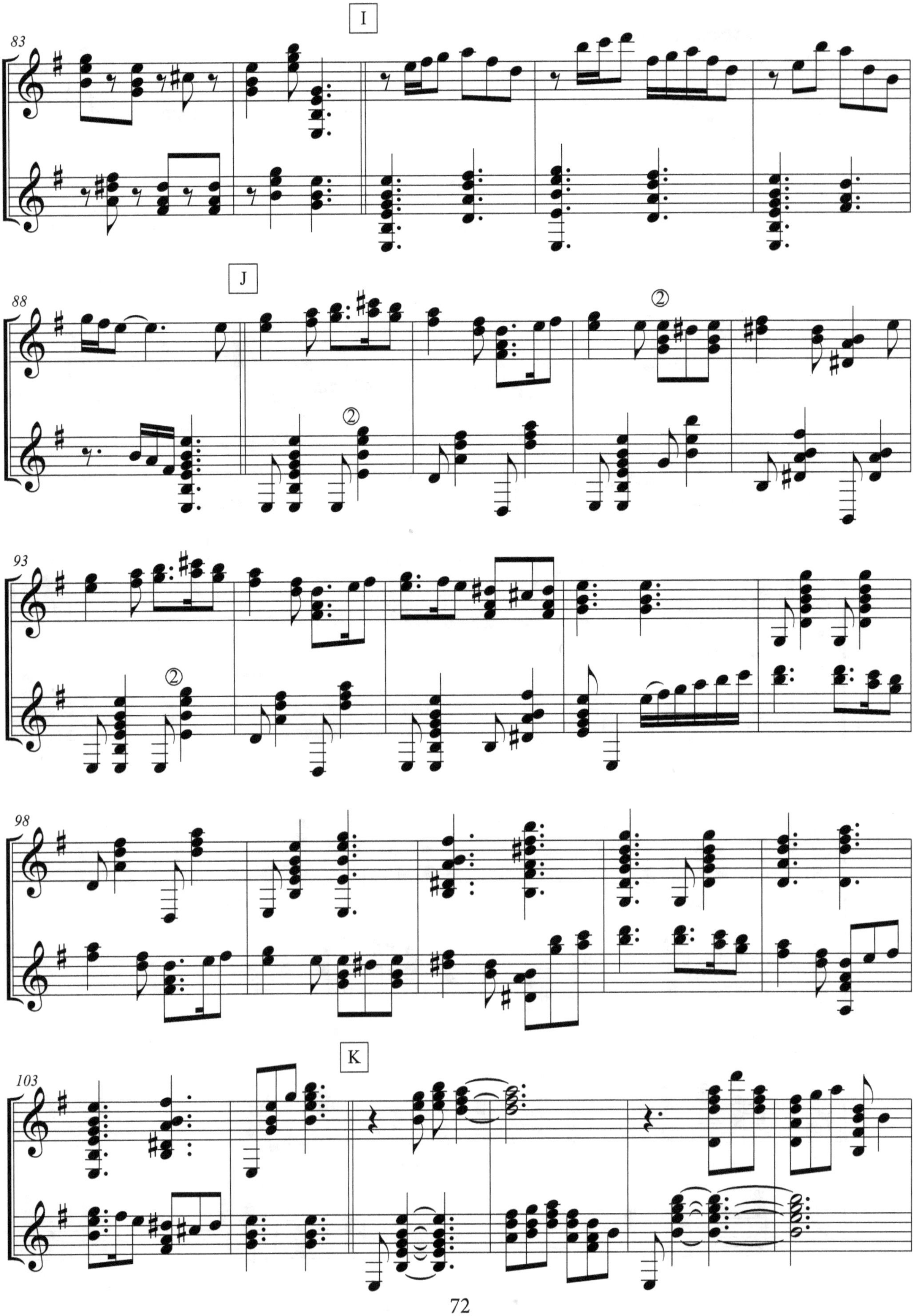
I
83
J
88
②
②
93
②
98
K
103

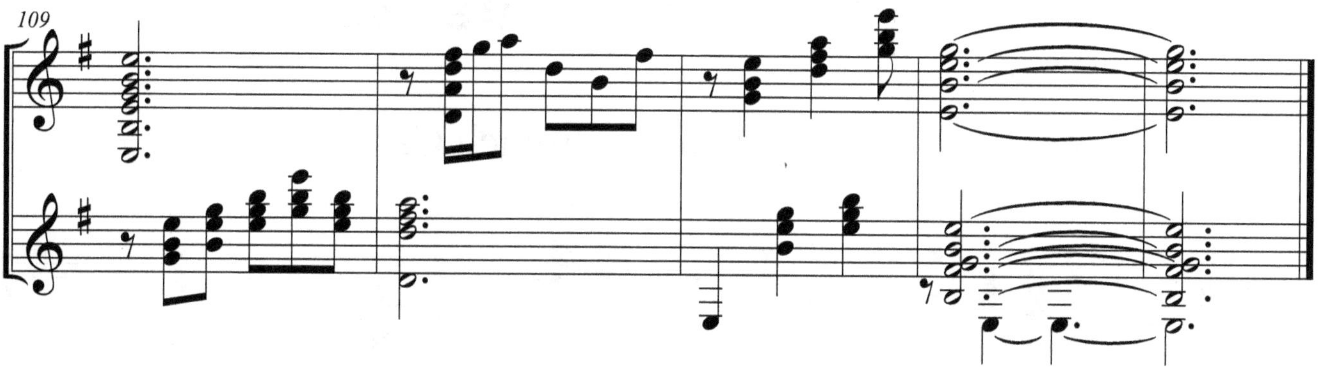
109

Gaudete, Christus Est Natus

Medieval French Carol

William Bay

Spirited ♩ = 120

Single note melody 1st time through

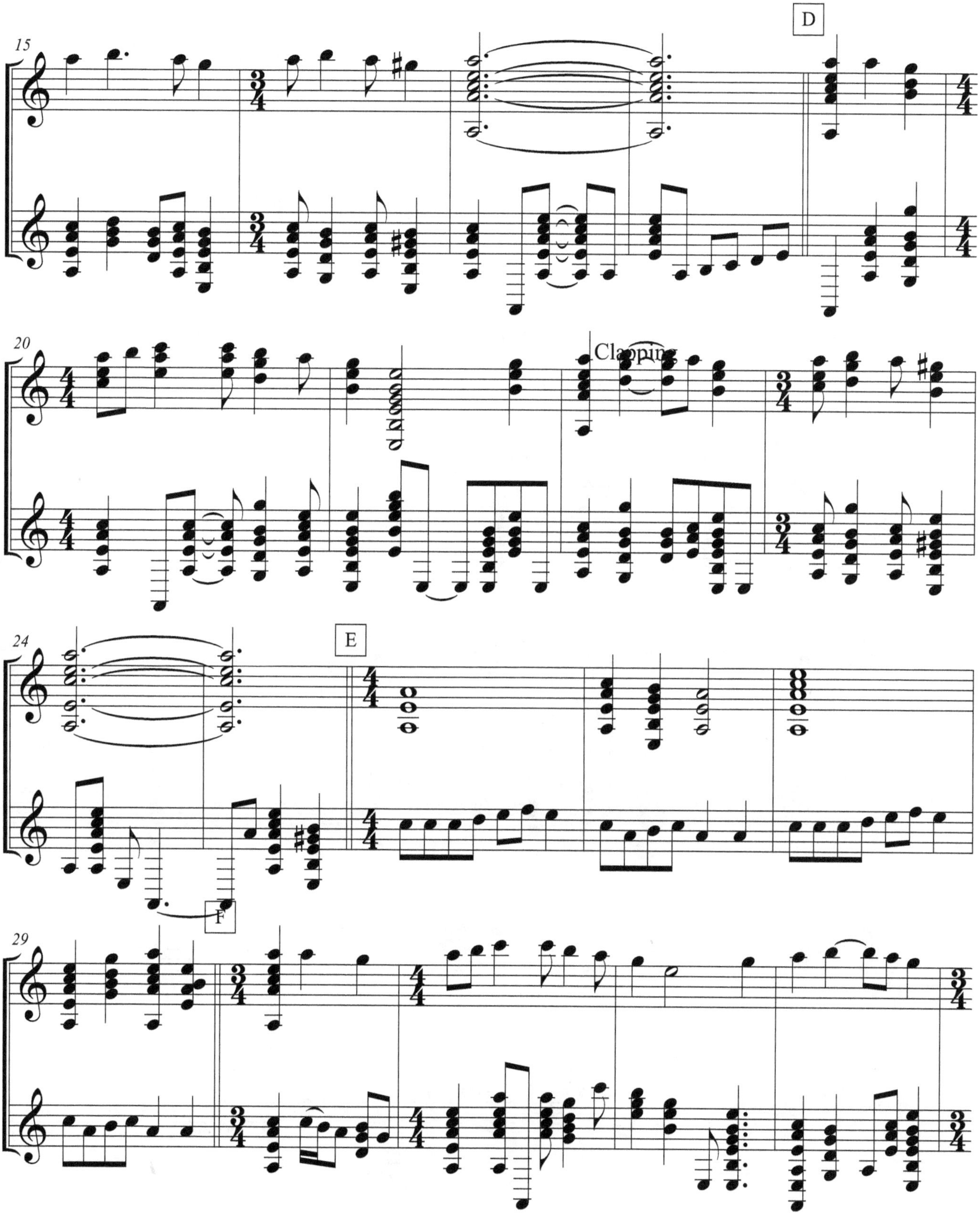
D
Clapping
E
F

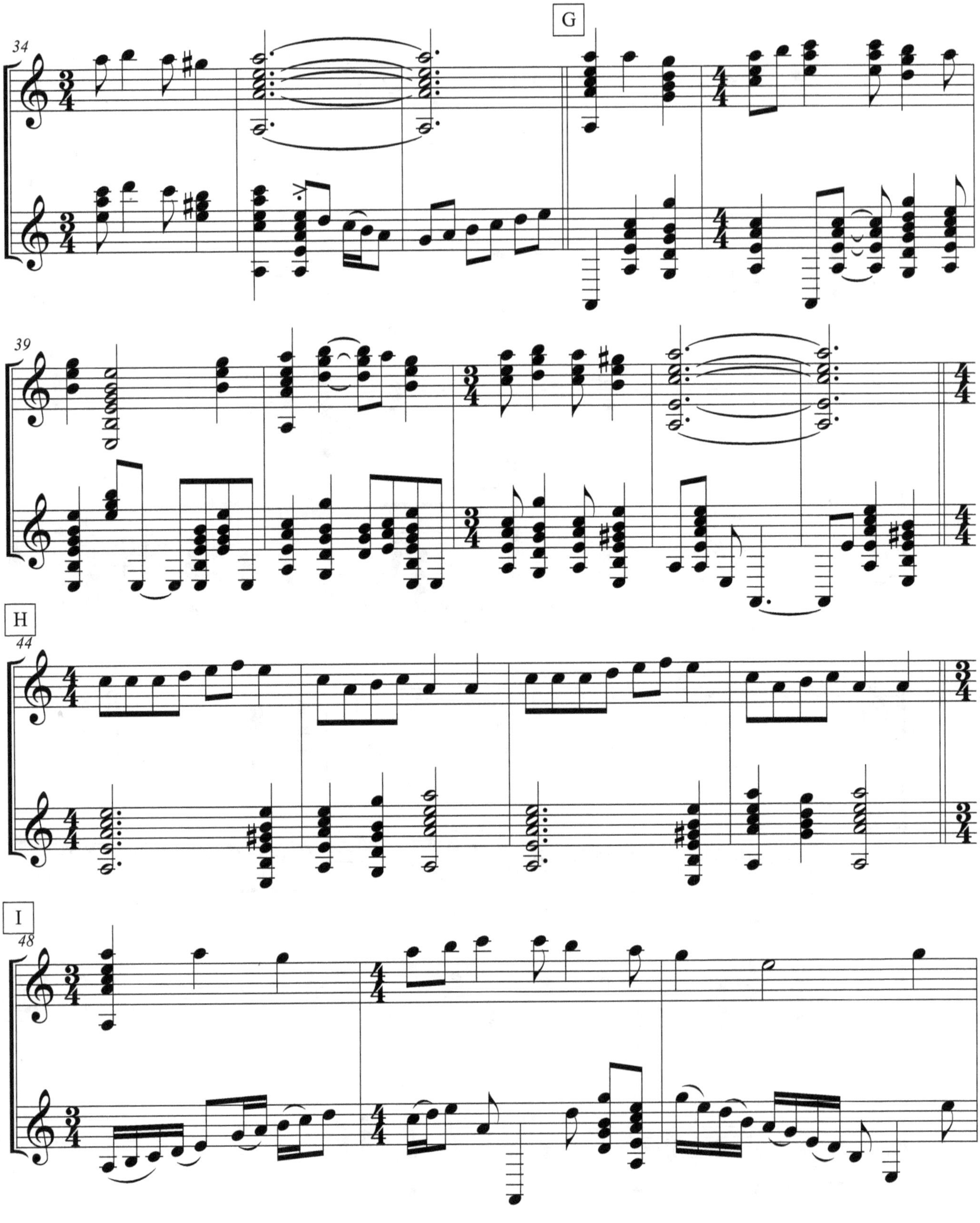
34
G
39
H
44
I
48

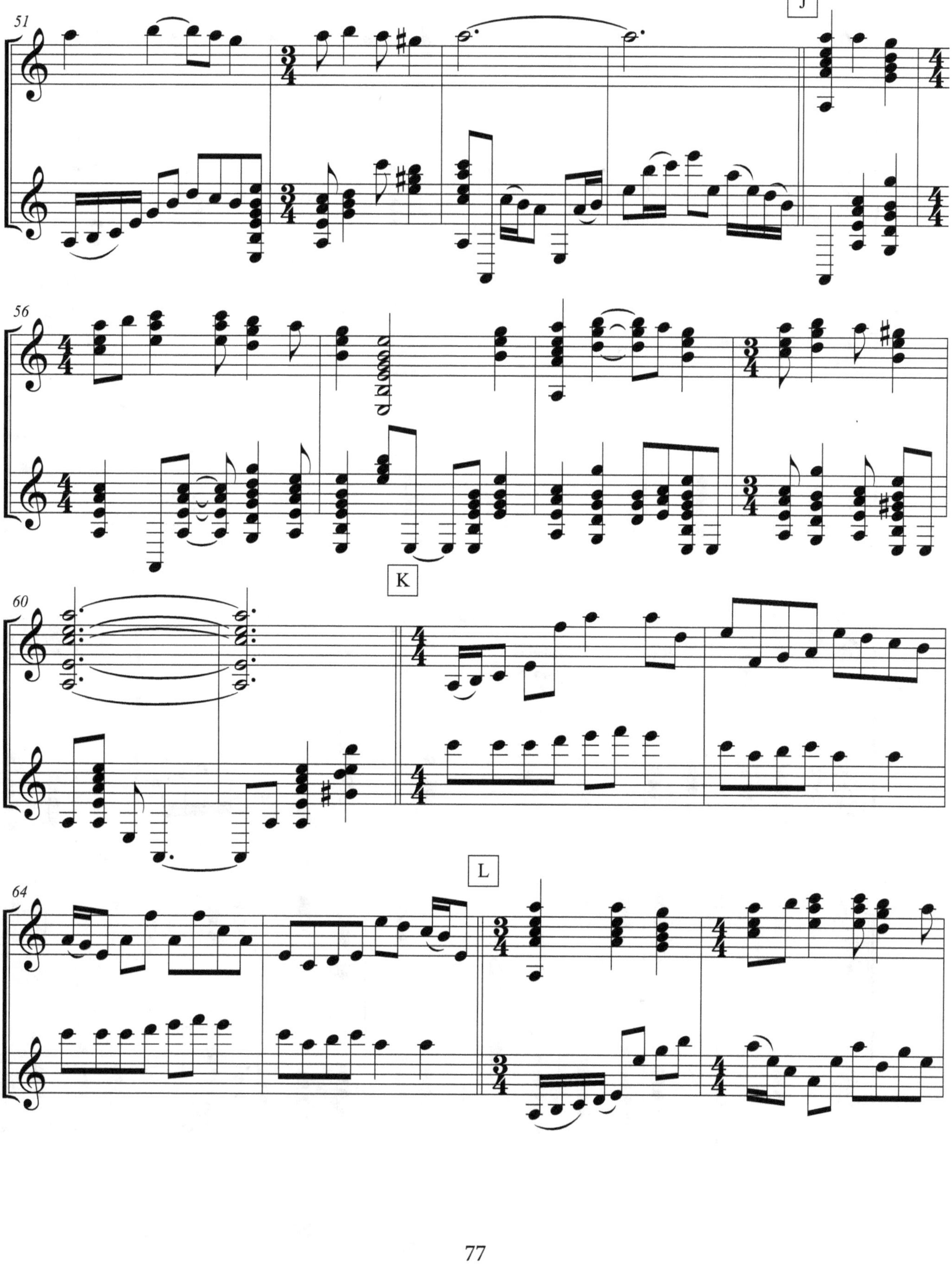
51
J
56
60
K
64
L

Clapping

M

N

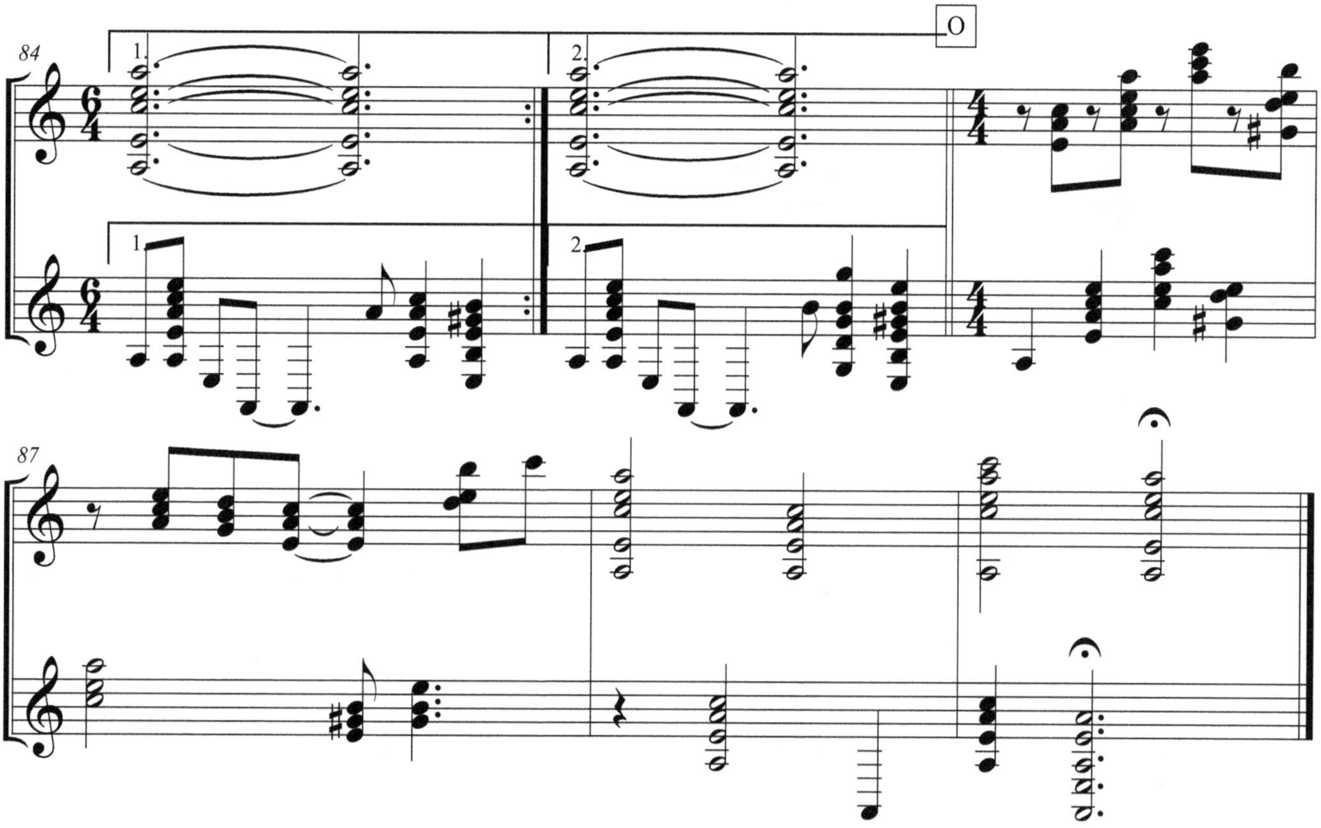
84
1.
2.
O
87

Lullay, My Liking

15th Century England

Musical Setting by William Bay

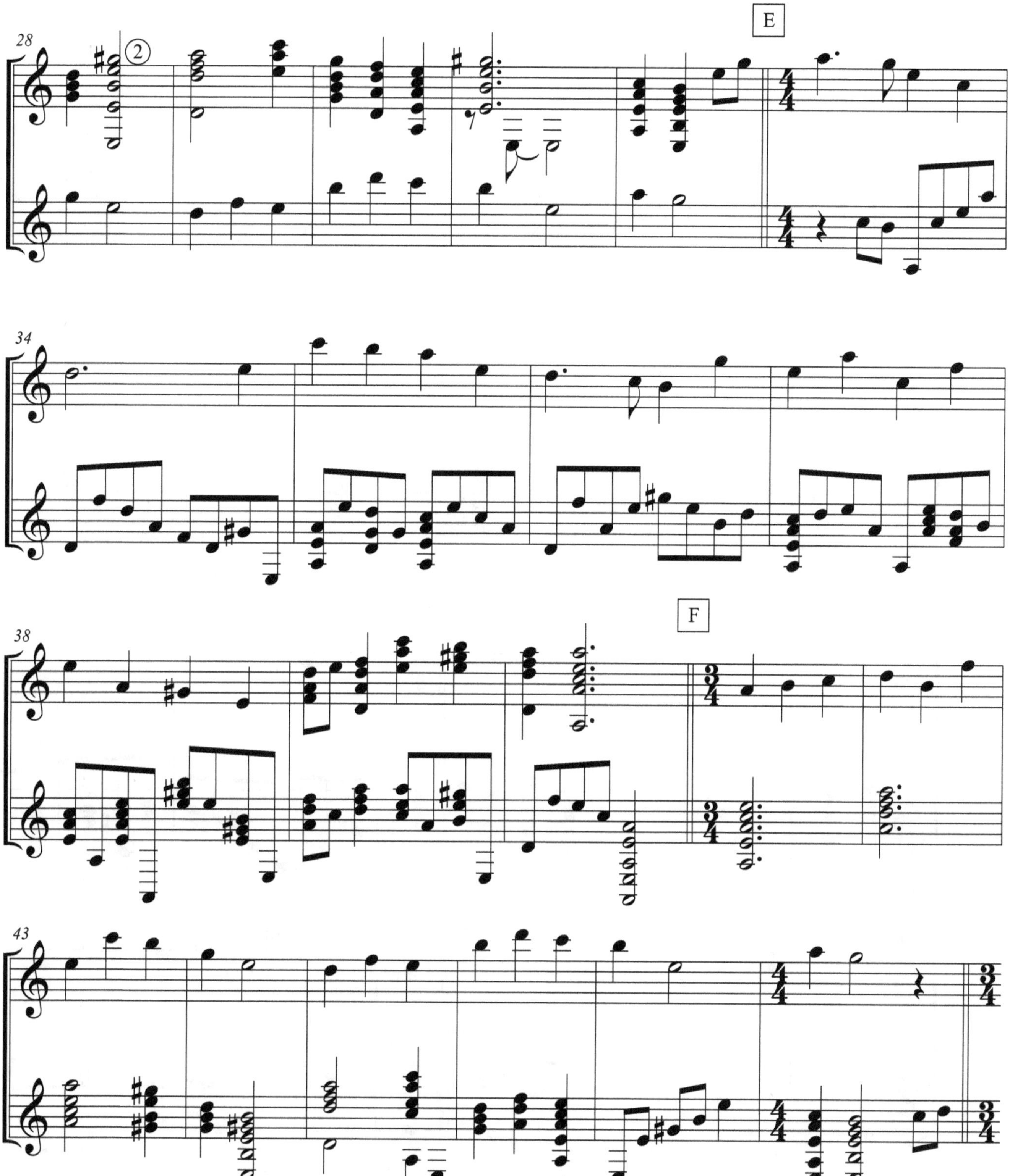
28
②
E
34
38
F
43

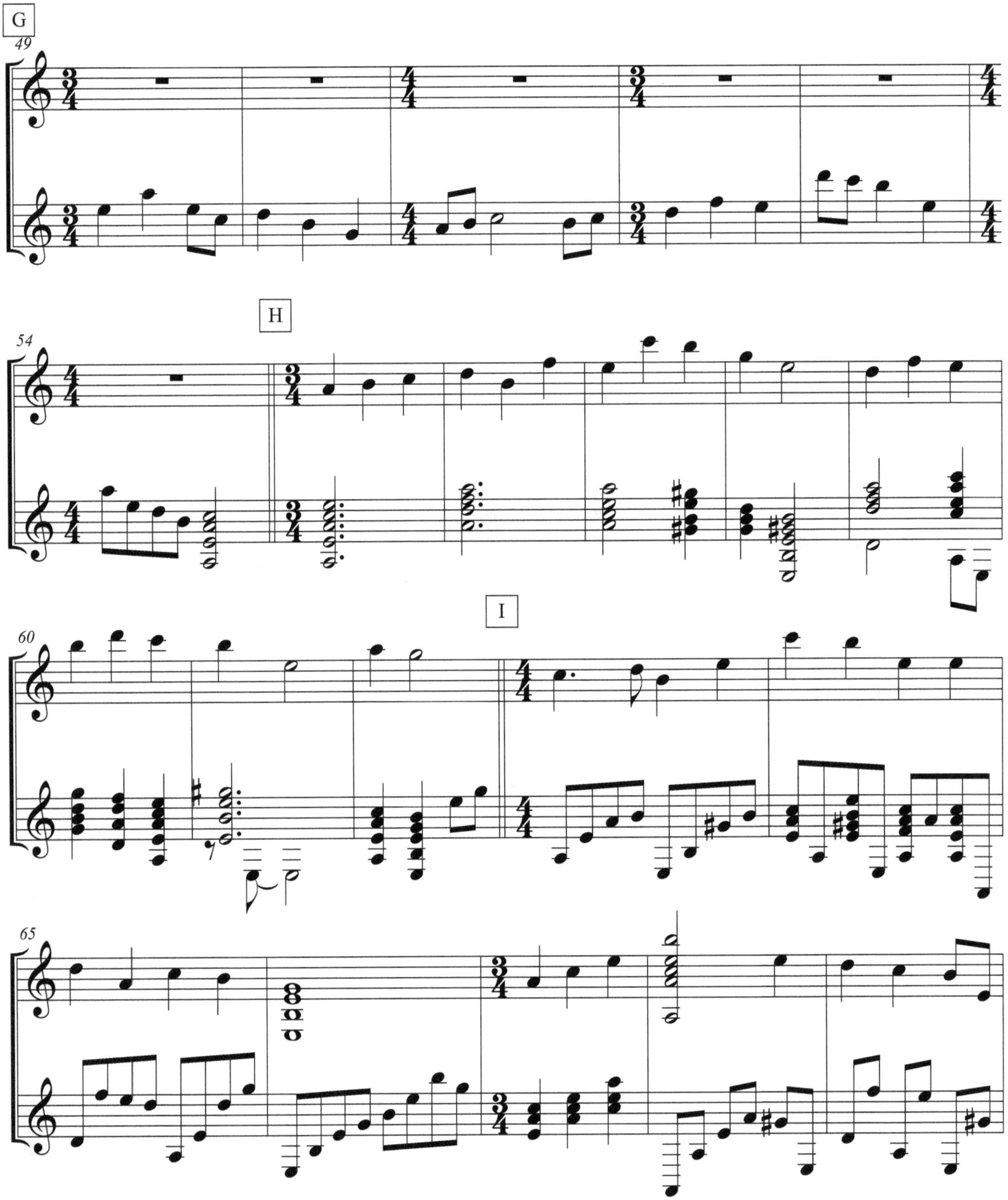
G
49
54
H
60
I
65

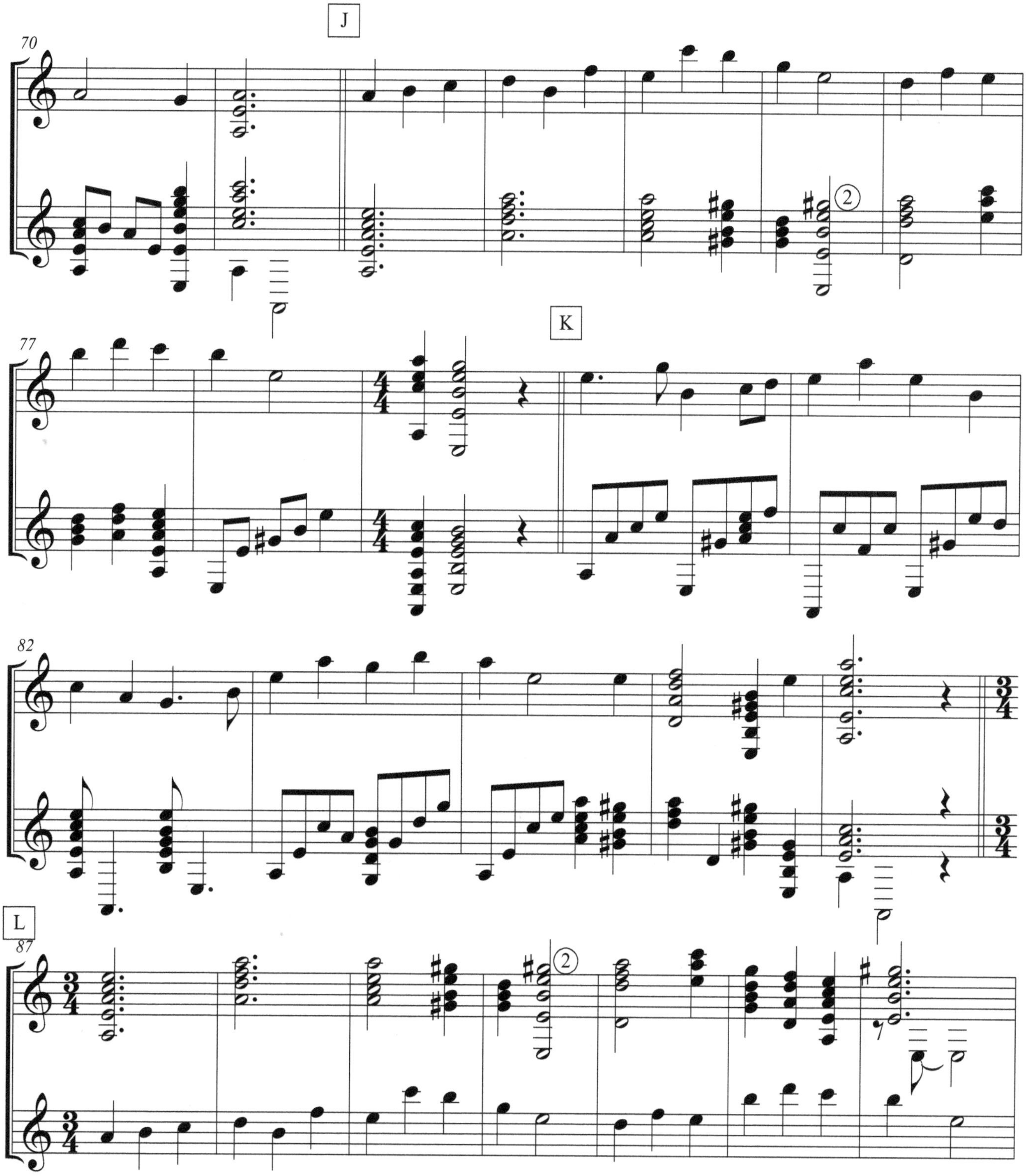
70
J
77
K
82
L
87
2

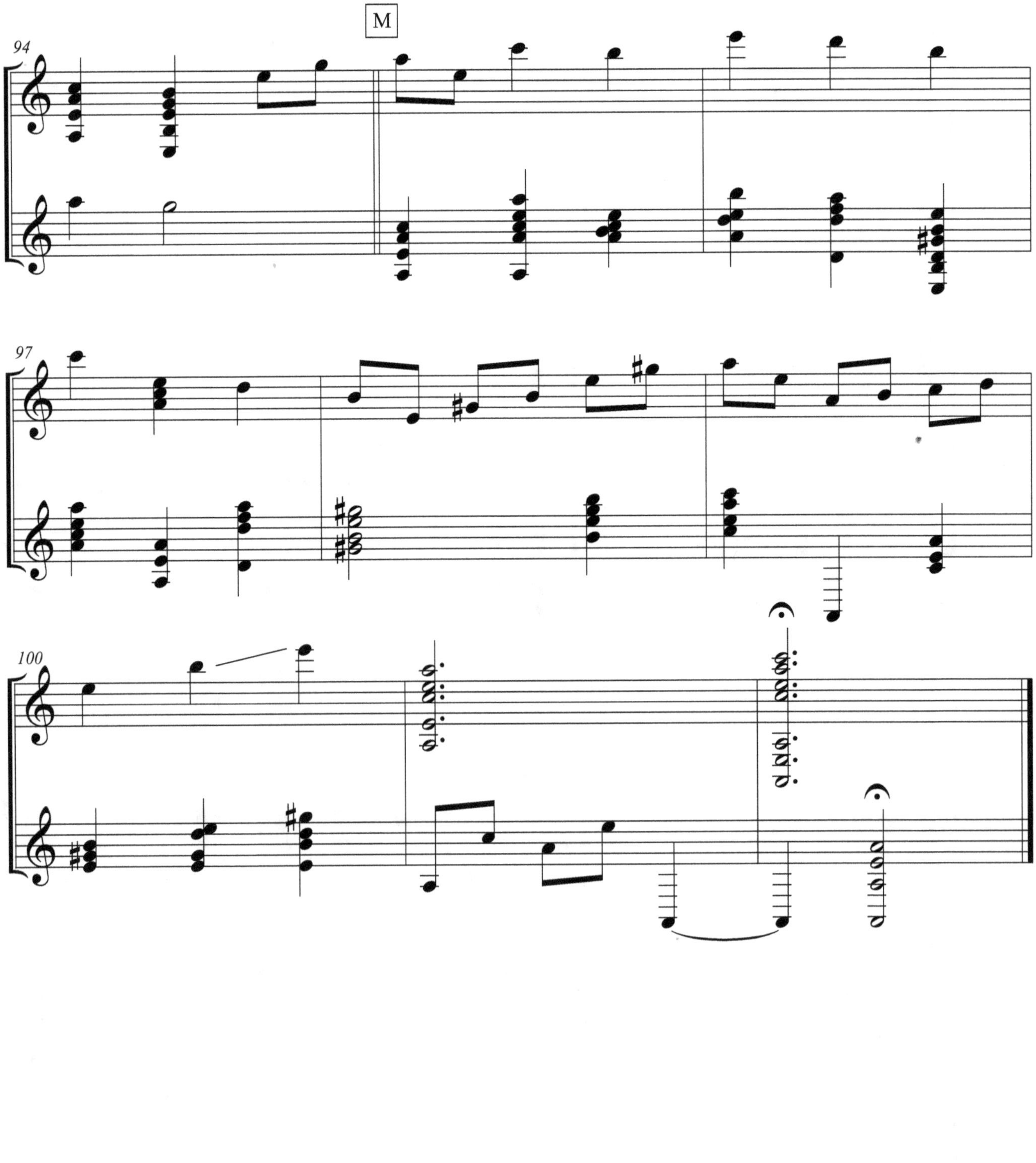
M
94
97
100

www.ingramcontent.com/pod-product-compliance
Lightning Source LLC
Chambersburg PA
CBHW062052090426
42740CB00016B/3107